Gun Control

by Jenny MacKay

LUCENT BOOKS
A part of Gale, Cengage Learning

GALE
CENGAGE Learning·

Detroit • New York • San Francisco • New Haven, Conn • Waterville, Maine • London

LIBRARY OF CONGRESS CATALOGING-IN-PUBLICATION DATA

MacKay, Jenny, 1978-
   Gun control / by Jenny MacKay.
      pages cm. -- (Hot topics)
   Includes bibliographical references and index.
   ISBN 978-1-4205-0815-4 (hardcover)
  1. Gun control--United States--Juvenile literature. 2. Firearms ownership--United States--Juvenile literature. I. Title.
   HV7436.M325 2013
   363.330973--dc23

                    2012047682

Lucent Books
27500 Drake Rd.
Farmington Hills, MI 48331

ISBN-13: 978-1-4205-0815-4
ISBN-10: 1-4205-0815-6

Printed in the United States of America
1 2 3 4 5 6 7 17 16 15 14 13

CONTENTS

FOREWORD   **4**

INTRODUCTION   **6**
Murder by Gunfire

CHAPTER 1   **9**
Guns and the Law in U.S. History

CHAPTER 2   **25**
Legal Issues in the Gun Control Debate

CHAPTER 3   **41**
Arguments in Favor of Gun Control

CHAPTER 4   **58**
Arguments in Favor of Gun Rights

CHAPTER 5   **75**
The Gun Control Battle Rages On

NOTES   **91**

DISCUSSION QUESTIONS   **97**

ORGANIZATIONS TO CONTACT   **99**

FOR MORE INFORMATION   **103**

INDEX   **105**

PICTURE CREDITS   **111**

ABOUT THE AUTHOR   **112**

FOREWORD

Young people today are bombarded with information. Aside from traditional sources such as newspapers, television, and the radio, they are inundated with a nearly continuous stream of data from electronic media. They send and receive e-mails and instant messages, read and write online "blogs," participate in chat rooms and forums, and surf the web for hours. This trend is likely to continue. As Patricia Senn Breivik, the former dean of university libraries at Wayne State University in Detroit, has stated, "Information overload will only increase in the future. By 2020, for example, the available body of information is expected to double every 73 days! How will these students find the information they need in this coming tidal wave of information?"

Ironically, this overabundance of information can actually impede efforts to understand complex issues. Whether the topic is abortion, the death penalty, gay rights, or obesity, the deluge of fact and opinion that floods the print and electronic media is overwhelming. The news media report the results of polls and studies that contradict one another. Cable news shows, talk radio programs, and newspaper editorials promote narrow viewpoints and omit facts that challenge their own political biases. The World Wide Web is an electronic minefield where legitimate scholars compete with the postings of ordinary citizens who may or may not be well-informed or capable of reasoned argument. At times, strongly worded testimonials and opinion pieces both in print and electronic media are presented as factual accounts.

Conflicting quotes and statistics can confuse even the most diligent researchers. A good example of this is the question of whether or not the death penalty deters crime. For instance, one study found that murders decreased by nearly one-third when the death penalty was reinstated in New York in 1995. Death penalty supporters cite this finding to support their argument that the existence of the death penalty deters criminals from committing murder. However, another study found that states without the death penalty have murder rates below the national average. This study is cited by opponents of capital punishment, who reject the claim that the death penalty deters murder. Students need context and clear, informed discussion if they are to think critically and make informed decisions.

The Hot Topics series is designed to help young people wade through the glut of fact, opinion, and rhetoric so that they can think critically about controversial issues. Only by reading and thinking critically will they be able to formulate a viewpoint that is not simply the parroted views of others. Each volume of the series focuses on one of today's most pressing social issues and provides a balanced overview of the topic. Carefully crafted narrative, fully documented primary and secondary source quotes, informative sidebars, and study questions all provide excellent starting points for research and discussion. Full-color photographs and charts enhance all volumes in the series. With its many useful features, the Hot Topics series is a valuable resource for young people struggling to understand the pressing issues of the modern era.

INTRODUCTION

MURDER BY GUNFIRE

On the morning of January 8, 2011, Arizona representative Gabrielle Giffords was holding a Congress on Your Corner event outside a supermarket in Tucson, Arizona, when a man ran toward her, pulled out a pistol, and shot her in the head. He shot eighteen more people before trying to run from the scene. Bystanders tackled him and held him down until police arrived. Meanwhile, Giffords lay unconscious alongside the other wounded people. Six victims died in the attack, including one of Giffords's staff members, a U.S. district judge, and a nine-year-old girl.

The incident launched national debate about political bipartisanship (Giffords was a Democrat in a largely Republican state), but most controversy in the wake of the shooting was about gun control. The gunman, twenty-two-year-old Jared Loughner, had a history of drug abuse and had displayed many signs of a serious mental illness in the years leading up to his rampage. The U.S. Army had denied him entrance because he admitted to frequent drug use. Pima Community College had dismissed him as a student because he repeatedly exhibited signs of mental illness that disturbed and even frightened his classmates and instructors. He had been arrested for drug-related offenses and property vandalism. He had even posted videos on the Internet of himself discussing violent topics.

Gun control advocates used the case to back their claims that the nation needs more-effective laws regulating who can purchase a firearm. In the months preceding the attack, Loughner had purchased from legal gun sellers a shotgun and the semiautomatic 9mm pistol he used in his shooting spree. He passed a background check for both purchases, despite factors that should have disqualified him from owning a gun: He had a criminal record, a history of drug abuse, and documented evidence that he might have a mental illness. According to gun control laws, any of those things can bar a person from legally owning a gun.

Further fueling the arguments of gun control supporters was the fact that Arizona has some of the most lenient gun laws in the nation. Critics of lax gun laws said the tragedy might have been prevented if there were more laws restricting gun ownership, such as a requirement for the military to report to the Federal Bureau of Investigation (FBI) anyone like Loughner that it refuses to enlist due to drug abuse. "Had this reporting requirement been in place, Loughner would likely have been prevented from purchasing a firearm,"[1] said Senator Chuck Schumer of New York.

Emergency personnel attend shooting victims outside a shopping center in Tucson, Arizona, on January 8, 2011. U.S. representative Gabrielle Giffords was critically wounded along with eighteen other people, of which six, including a child, died. The incident renewed the gun control controversy in the United States.

Gun rights supporters fired back. They blamed inadequate record keeping by law enforcement agencies, saying that what the nation needed was better enforcement of existing laws, not new or more restrictive laws against gun ownership. "It doesn't need to be any more illegal than it already is to shoot a Congresswoman in the head,"[2] said Charles Heller of the Arizona Citizens Defense League.

Ironically, even though most Democrats typically favor stricter gun control laws, Giffords was a Democrat who supported gun rights and her state's lenient gun policies. Her shooting came to symbolize the partisan bickering that traditionally accompanies discussions of gun control. Had she supported the usual Democratic notions on stricter gun control and managed to change Arizona's gun policies, Giffords's shooter might never have been able to obtain his weapons. On the other hand, he clearly intended to hurt and kill people and might have found a way to do so even without guns.

In the end, Giffords, though permanently disabled by the traumatic brain injury, miraculously survived being shot through the head. The incident gave new life to gun control arguments that had been quiet for years—issues like the Second Amendment, background checks, the availability of semiautomatic handguns, political partisanship in gun control, and the very real danger that guns can pose when a person with bad intentions gets his or her hands on one.

CHAPTER 1

GUNS AND THE LAW
IN U.S. HISTORY

Firearms and the right to own and use them are among the most debated topics in the United States today. Arguments position public safety against the rights of private citizens, and both sides have strong opinions. Beliefs about gun control have become a political marker for Democrats and Republicans, and political elections often become battlegrounds between those in favor of and those opposed to the personal possession of firearms. Opinions about gun control divide the United States politically and socially.

The gun debate, however, is not new. For as long as the United States has been a nation, its people have argued about firearms—who should have them and what legal controls should be placed on them. For early Americans, firearms were indispensable tools for hunting and self-defense, but even before the United States became a country, American colonists were sometimes at odds about whether guns were a good idea in the new land. The debate about these deadly weapons is deeply rooted in American history and culture.

Early Firepower and Controversy

Firearms existed long before the first Europeans came to America. Historians believe firepower originated in about A.D. 300 in ancient China. Chinese inventors wrote about the discovery of a powder that exploded when exposed to flame. Recipes for making the powder eventually migrated to Europe during trading expeditions. In the mid-1200s Europeans experimented with new ways to use the explosive powder, and by the 1340s the cannon had become a potent weapon. It consisted of a thick iron tube sealed at one end and open at the other. Someone loaded gunpowder into the sealed end and then rolled in a large ball of lead. A gunman lit a fuse to ignite the powder. The resulting explosion propelled the lead ball out of the tube with enough force to topple the turret on a castle wall or leave a gaping hole in a rival ship.

Cannons were standard wartime weapons in the Middle Ages, but their size and weight limited their usefulness. In the late 1300s people in Italy and England invented miniature, handheld cannons, which became known as "hand guns." These worked by the same principle as cannons, requiring the user to add gunpowder to the barrel and insert a small lead ball. The powder in the gun had to be ignited by a match or a small fuse before the bullet would be discharged. Using a match meant the shooter had only one hand free to steady the gun. Using a fuse freed both hands so the shooter could stabilize the weapon, but fuses caused a delay between lighting the flame and firing the shot, and in rainy weather, fuses could be extinguished before the gun fired. Early handguns were difficult to use, hard to aim, and limited in range—they could shoot a bullet only 30 to 40 yards (27m to 37m).

In the 1400s guns were modernized with a spring-loaded mechanism to strike a piece of flint, or stone, against a strip of iron. The movement shaved off a speck of flaming iron that dropped into the gunpowder. Guns could now be shot with a tug of a spring-loaded trigger. Both hands steadied the weapon, which made it more accurate. Bullets were expelled with enough force to pierce not only armor but animal hide. Handguns became popular in Europe for battles, self-defense, and hunting. In 1690 the British began mass-producing various closely related pistols patterned after an original model called the Brown Bess. These became the standard guns used by the British army for the next century. Says sociologist Gregg Lee Carter, "The efficient use of the Bess, in fact, put the British regulars among the most effective and feared troops of the period."[3]

The effectiveness and power of guns made them popular but controversial among Europeans, and especially the British, who had the world's most sophisticated and powerful national military. Some British subjects were concerned about the killing ability of handguns, but others saw guns as necessary tools to protect themselves from the army of any king who might want to control his people. In 1689 the British passed the English Bill of Rights, which granted the people certain freedoms and protections. One of those protections read, "Subjects which are

A seventeenth-century soldier with his arquebus, an early form of a matchlock rifle, which used a burning fuse, or match, to ignite the powder.

Protestants may have arms for their defense suitable to their conditions, and as allowed by law."[4] An armed citizenry would be able to stand up to foes, even a tyrannical king.

A Right to Firearms

The British belief in an armed citizenry spread overseas to the new British colonies in North America. Guns were necessary tools in the new land, used for hunting and self-defense against hostile Native Americans. The colonists, like the citizens of their

A statue of a minuteman militia member commemorates the milita of Massachusetts. The minutemen (so called because of their readiness) were the first Americans to fight in the Revolutionary War.

homeland, were wary of a powerful king who could command an armed military to control the people. They eventually faced off against exactly such a ruler when they united against King George III in the 1770s, declared themselves an independent country, and went to war against Britain's powerful military. The newborn United States of America had no money for a large national army. Its fighting forces during the Revolutionary War consisted largely of a militia of private citizens who brought their guns from home.

FAR FROM EXTINCT

"Undoubtedly some think that the Second Amendment is outmoded in a society where our standing army is the pride of our nation. . . . What is not debatable is that it is not the role of this court to pronounce the Second Amendment extinct."—Antonin Scalia, U.S. Supreme Court justice

Quoted in Bill Mears. "High Court Strikes Down Gun Ban." CNN, June 26, 2008. http://articles.cnn.com/2008-06-26/us/scotus.guns_1_gun-ban-second-amendment-gun-violence?_s=PM:US.

The untrained militia was poorly suited for war. Most militia soldiers had little or no formal battle training, and although they had guns, many were not experts at using them. Nevertheless, after years of vicious fighting, the United States won its freedom from Britain. It then faced the task of establishing a government and a constitution, and one of the most pressing controversies was what to do about national defense. Some citizens thought guns were dangerous in the hands of untrained users and best suited for professional soldiers in a national army. Others believed allowing private citizens to own firearms guaranteed that the new government could never overpower its people. In 1791 the authors of the U.S. Constitution drafted the Bill of Rights, a list of amendments that clarified the original Constitution from two years earlier. "Fearing federal control—even use of state militias against rebellious citizens—anti-federalists insisted on the Second Amendment,"[5] say law professor H. Richard Uviller and historian William G. Merkel. The amendment was worded: "A well-regulated militia being necessary to the security of a free State, the right of the people to keep and bear arms shall not be infringed." Under the protection of this Second Amendment, American citizens have practiced their right to manufacture, purchase, and use firearms ever since.

Gun Evolution

The Second Amendment right to keep and bear arms, including guns, is a fundamental part of American history, but it also has caused considerable problems for the American people. Gun manufacturers continually make weapons even more accurate and lethal. Rampant gun violence has been a mainstay of several famous eras of U.S. development and has led to numerous calls for regulation of firearms.

As the United States expanded westward throughout the 1800s, the western frontier became a vast area of cattle ranches, scattered towns, and widespread lawlessness. Guns accompanied cowboys and outlaws into this Wild West, especially the popular six shooter—a pistol that held six bullets in a revolving ammunition cartridge. Many westerners had holsters attached to their belts for carrying two such handguns with them at all times. Arguments that erupted on streets or saloons sometimes ended in dangerous exchanges of gunfire.

Many citizens of the Wild West demanded regulation of firearms, at least within towns and cities. Some towns were incorporated mainly so the citizens could form a local governing body with the authority to forbid people to carry or shoot guns in the town. New towns also hired sheriffs and deputies to keep peace in the streets. The hot-headed pistol wielders of the Wild West brought about some of the earliest arguments in favor of regulating Americans' right to carry guns wherever they went. "Ironically, and contrary to legend, gun laws did more to settle the West than did guns,"[6] says Carter.

Guns in the City

The Wild West was not the only region of the United States where people tired of gun violence and demanded regulation. Big cities had their own problems with guns. In 1920 the U.S.

government banned the production, sale, and transportation of all kinds of alcoholic beverages in the United States, a law called Prohibition. Criminal gangs took over the illegal production, smuggling, and sale of alcoholic beverages to consumers. These gangs battled one another viciously, trying to gain an advantage over competitors and make more money in the alcohol trade. American cities, especially Chicago and New York, saw gun violence of a magnitude never before experienced in the nation.

Frightening new advancements in gun technology during Prohibition included the Thompson submachine gun, or Tommy gun. This rifle-style firearm could rapidly expel twenty to thirty bullets between reloadings. In the hands of gang members, Tommy guns terrorized city streets. Mass murders and drive-by shootings—assassinations from within moving cars—became a public menace. "Competing organized crime groups engaged in spectacular assassinations and shootouts in public," says constitutional law professor James B. Jacobs. "The media and the public demanded a response."[7]

In 1933, realizing Prohibition had sent crime spiraling out of control, the U.S. government repealed the ban on alcohol. It also made weapons like the Tommy gun scarce by passing the National Firearms Act in 1934 and the Federal Firearms Act in 1938. These laws required gun dealers to be licensed in order to sell weapons, put restrictions on the transfer of guns across state lines, and heavily taxed the possession of machine guns

In the 1920s and 1930s the gangster's gun of choice was the Thompson submachine gun. In 1934 the National Firearms Act banned its use.

among private citizens. Thus, government control of alcohol ended at about the same time modern government control of firearms began.

Ironically, even though Prohibition brought public out- cry for more regulation of guns, it also created a compelling argument that more regulation of the firearms industry might backfire. Just as people still obtained and used alcohol during Prohibition, opponents of gun control said people would still obtain and use guns if they were outlawed. Many supporters of gun rights in America today argue that the lawlessness and gang power that prevailed during Prohibition would only be repeated if the government were to institute a similar ban on guns. "Pro- hibition did not eliminate alcohol sales or consumption," says political science professor Harry L. Wilson. "Can we reason- ably expect greater restrictions on firearms to reduce crime?"[8] Despite concern that gun control efforts might only echo the failure of alcohol prohibition, however, the 1930s were not the last time American citizens would call for restrictions on firearm possession.

Uncivilized Weapons in the Civil Rights Era

A decade after Prohibition ended, the United States fought in World War II. A sense of national patriotism marked the era. Violent crime rates were low, and public calls for additional gun control faded. After the war was over, however, the United States became the site of a new kind of war: a public struggle for equal rights for its black citizens. The civil rights movement of the 1960s was marked by considerable violence. Churches were bombed. Vehicles and buildings were set on fire. People assaulted one another and each other's property. The most vivid, tragic interpersonal attacks of the era were crimes committed with guns.

Cities saw a tremendous increase in murders during the civil rights movement, and guns were the primary weapons being used. From 1964 to 1968, gun homicides increased 89 percent in the United States. In part as a reaction to the fear of being shot in their own neighborhoods, American citizens took part in a huge gun-buying spree. The nation's gun sales quadrupled,

Gun Control as Racism

Some of the earliest efforts at gun control were actually efforts to control certain ethnic groups by disarming them. Early in the nation's history, white people passed laws to prohibit free black people from having guns. Even after the Civil War, many states continued to enforce these laws. In the late 1800s European immigrants arrived in the United States by the millions and were linked to crime waves in cities. Local governments responded by enacting gun control measures that required a permit to obtain a firearm and then refusing to grant permits to immigrants. During the civil rights movement of the 1960s, the white supremacist group known as the Ku Klux Klan favored gun control measures that banned cheap handguns because poor Americans, especially poor black Americans, often could not afford more expensive firearms they could have used to defend themselves from racial attacks. Even today, taxing guns or ammunition, prohibiting sales of inexpensive handguns, and charging high registration fees for firearms are seen as ways to make guns accessible only to certain classes and to prevent the poor from exercising their Second Amendment right.

from 600,000 gun purchases in 1964 to 2.4 million in 1968. Firearms could be ordered through the mail in those days, making it impossible for law enforcement to keep track of who was buying guns.

Americans widely blamed the lenient or nonexistent regulation of weapons in the 1960s for three of the most infamous crimes of the twentieth century. The shooting deaths of President John Kennedy in November 1963, civil rights leader Martin Luther King Jr. in April 1968, and Senator Robert Kennedy in June 1968 increased the public outcry about the ease of obtaining firearms. President Kennedy's assumed assassin, Lee Harvey Oswald, received the rifle he allegedly used in the murder by mail order using a false name. King's assassin, James Earl Ray, was a convicted armed robber and prison escapee who was legally banned from having firearms like the rifle he used in the assassination. Senator Kennedy's killer, Palestinian immigrant Sirhan Sirhan, used a handgun in his crime, a weapon that American citizens increasingly disliked because its primary purpose was to shoot at other people—not, as could be said of rifles and shotguns, to be used in sports like hunting.

Renewed Call to Control Guns

The high-profile shootings of the 1960s became the basis for new gun legislation. Says historian Duncan Watts, "The Gun Control Act (1968) was passed following the assassinations of Martin Luther King and Robert Kennedy, when elected officials were aware of a widespread public mood to curb gun ownership."[9] The act consisted of a group of federal laws that made gun purchase or possession illegal for minors under age eighteen, convicted felons, anyone with a drug record, or anyone

The June 1968 assassination of Robert Kennedy, shown, as well as the assassination of Martin Luther King Jr. just two months prior, spawned the Gun Control Act of 1968, which gave the government a better system for monitoring gun sales and gun possession in the United States.

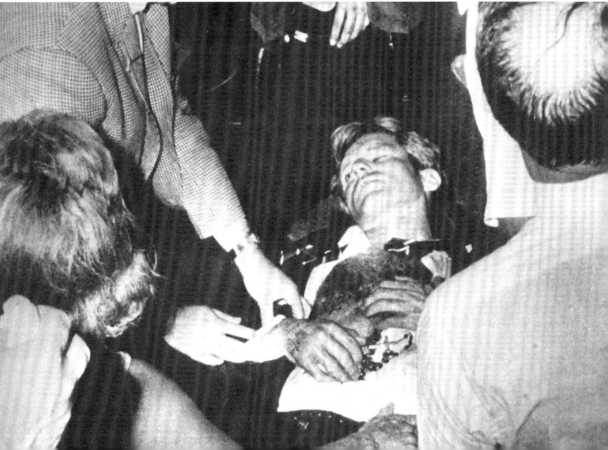

with documented treatment for a mental health problem. The new law also banned mail-order gun purchases and other methods of gun sales that crossed state borders, which made it easier to regulate who was buying and selling guns. Guns were given serial numbers to make individual weapons easier to track, and gun dealers, who now had to be federally licensed, were required to keep records of all gun sales and buyers.

JUDGMENT CALLS

"Concealed carry is not for folks who lack good judgment and restraint. Even a right must be exercised responsibly, and carrying a gun is a grave responsibility."—Bruce N. Elmer, National Rifle Association certified law enforcement instructor

Bruce N. Elmer. *Armed: The Essential Guide to Concealed Carry.* Iola, WI: Gun Digest, 2012, p. 83.

The Gun Control Act of 1968 gave the federal government a better system for monitoring gun sales and possession in the United States, but it was unpopular with lawmakers and citizens who disliked the government's move to stretch its power over the states. "Gun rights supporters began almost immediately to press for legislation that would weaken or repeal the 1968 gun control laws, which they viewed as excessive and grossly unfair to law-abiding sportsmen,"[10] says public policy professor Kristin A. Goss. To add to its growing unpopularity, the Gun Control Act also did not eliminate or even significantly reduce gun violence in the United States. Instead, the FBI reported that gun homicide rates increased steadily in the first five years after the new laws were passed. A decade after the Gun Control Act, gun violence in America was more widespread than ever. Firearms caused the deaths of almost as many people as car accidents did. The Gun Control Act had given the government more power to oversee firearms, their owners, and their sellers and buyers, but it had apparently done nothing to prevent gun violence.

An Assassin Strikes Again

On March 30, 1981, the country witnessed another assassination attempt against a president. Ronald Reagan was waving to spectators on a sidewalk in Washington, D.C., when John Hinckley Jr., a member of the crowd, drew a revolver and fired six shots at him. One bullet entered Reagan's chest, puncturing his lung and narrowly missing his heart. Bullets also struck security officer Thomas Delahanty and White House press secretary James Brady, who suffered a disabling head injury. Americans expressed alarm that Hinckley—a mentally troubled man who was ultimately found not guilty by reason of insanity—had so easily obtained and used a handgun to try to kill the president.

In the 1980s Brady and his wife, Sarah, became active in the Center to Prevent Handgun Violence and lobbied for the government to enact stricter gun control measures. In 1987 Congress considered a bill that would restrict gun purchases more than the 1968 Gun Control Act had done. It would require a waiting period between the time a gun was bought and the time the buyer could actually have it. During this period, police agencies would do a thorough background check on the buyer to see whether he or she was a convicted felon, had been diagnosed with a mental disorder, or was otherwise prohibited from owning a firearm. Under the Gun Control Act of 1968, formal background checks were not performed, and a customer could walk out of a store with a new weapon at the time of the purchase—something gun control supporters said was dangerous because the buyer might intend to go out and immediately shoot someone with the newly acquired weapon. Reagan himself supported the waiting period. "With the right to bear arms comes a great responsibility to use caution and common sense on handgun purchases," he said. "And it's just plain common sense that there be a waiting period to allow local law-enforcement officials to conduct background checks on those who wish to purchase handguns."[11]

Despite Reagan's support, some lawmakers still blocked the proposed legislation. For six years Congress debated stricter government control over firearms. Finally, in November 1993 lawmakers approved the Brady Handgun Violence Prevention Act, named after James and Sarah Brady, and President Bill Clinton signed it into law. The Brady Act, which went into effect in early 1994, required a waiting period of five business days between the purchase of a gun and the day the customer could actually have it. During this period, police had to confirm that the buyer was a legal U.S. citizen with no felony convictions, no known drug addiction, no diagnosed mental health disorder, and no dishonorable discharge from the military. The waiting-period requirement of the Brady Act expired five years later, in part because a national instant background check program could usually confirm in moments whether a buyer was legally cleared to own a gun, but background checks remained in place.

After he was wounded in the 1981 assassination attempt on President Ronald Reagan, James Brady and his wife, Sarah, pictured, became active in the Center to Prevent Handgun Violence.

The Aftermath of Gun Control

Gun control advocates saw the passing of the Brady Act as a major victory in the fight against gun violence. Although 1993 was a peak year for murder in the United States, by 1998, five years after the Brady Act was passed, the FBI reported that murder rates had dropped to their lowest point since 1967. However, researchers found that waiting periods and background checks for gun purchases had little if anything to do with the declining murder rate. Before the Brady Act, eighteen states had already required waiting periods and background checks for gun purchases. After the Brady Act, the remaining thirty-two states were forced to comply with the new rules. Gun crime rates fell at the same rate in both groups of states, suggesting that something besides the new, stricter law was causing the drop in crime rates. Furthermore, *all* violent crime in the United States declined at the same rate during this period, not just gun-related crime. Americans, it seemed, were more peaceful in general, which made it hard to determine whether stricter gun control had an impact on shootings at all.

As of 1994 the Center to Prevent Handgun Violence (a predecessor of the modern Brady Campaign to Prevent Gun Violence) claimed background checks had kept guns out of the hands of forty thousand buyers, a statistic widely touted as proving the success of the law. However, the act did nothing to address guns sold from dealers who had no license, which law enforcement experts pointed out was the way most criminals had always obtained their guns. People who could not pass the background check still got their hands on weapons; they just did it illegally from dealers who did not comply with background checks. "In retrospect we would not expect Brady to be effective against violent crime," said Philip Cook, a Duke University researcher who studied the consequences of the Brady Act. "Increasingly homicides are committed by career criminals who do not get their guns in legal ways."[12]

Another gun control measure met with similar assumed success in the years after it passed. In 1994 Clinton signed a ban on assault weapons, firearms designed specifically to harm or

The Nation's First Gun Control Organization

Today's Bureau of Alcohol, Tobacco, Firearms and Explosives initially belonged to the U.S. Department of the Treasury. Its roots go back to the 1790s, shortly after the Revolutionary War, when the government first imposed taxes on alcohol and tobacco and created a separate department with agents who caught tax evaders. During the nationwide prohibition of alcohol in the 1920s, the department had even greater responsibilities, which included catching alcohol smugglers. In the 1930s the country's problems with gangsters and guns prompted the government to add firearms to the department's responsibilities. It became known as the Bureau of Alcohol, Tobacco, and Firearms, or ATF. In the 1970s the government added explosives to things the ATF oversees. Today the ATF supports law enforcement agencies all over the country, helping with arson investigation, matching guns to the bullets fired from them, creating gang resistance education programs, and helping to investigate some of the most violent crimes in the nation. In 2003 the ATF became part of the U.S. Department of Justice. It is the government's official agency responsible for enforcing firearms laws in America.

The Bureau of Alcohol, Tobacco, Firearms, and Explosives (ATF) was formed in the 1790s to enforce the new laws levying taxes on alcohol and tobacco and, later, laws regulating firearms and explosives.

kill other people. Crime rates fell—but they had been on the decline throughout the 1990s, even before the ban. The ban was scheduled to sunset, or expire, after ten years. As the 2004 sunset date approached, many Americans worried that once the ban on assault weapons was lifted, the falling crime rate would be reversed and the country would see a dramatic rise in gun-related violence committed by assault weapons. However, once assault weapons were again legalized, crime rates only continued to drop, implying that the ban had had little effect on gun crime after all.

In 2011, seven years after the assault weapons ban was lifted, the national murder rate had dropped to half of what it was in 1991 and the lowest point in almost fifty years. The renewed availability of weapons considered highly dangerous did not lead to rampant shootings. Crime researchers have concluded that there is much more to violent crime in the United States than the mere presence or absence of guns. Nevertheless, supporters of both sides of the gun control argument continue to make strong cases in favor of their own position to allow or restrict weapons in the hands of Americans, keeping the debate over gun control active in modern government.

LEGAL ISSUES IN THE GUN CONTROL DEBATE

All three branches of the U.S. government have had a role in and been affected by gun control throughout history. The legislative branch, made up of the House of Representatives and the Senate, has the power to make new laws like the Gun Control Act of 1968 or the Brady Act of 1994. It also has the power to vote either to extend certain laws, like the ten-year Assault Weapons Ban of 1994, or let them expire. The executive branch, which consists of the president and his or her advisers, either signs the legislative branch's ideas into national law, as Bill Clinton did with the Brady Act, or denies legislation with a veto. The judicial branch, which consists of the federal court system headed by the Supreme Court, makes judgments about whether laws are allowed by the U.S. Constitution. Controversy over gun control affects government at all levels. Some of the most significant debates about firearms over the years, though, have fallen to the judicial branch and its interpretation of the Bill of Rights.

To Keep and Bear Arms

The Second Amendment, traditionally interpreted to mean that the government may not interfere with people's right to possess weapons, has long been the source of legal challenges. This single-sentence amendment impedes government efforts to prohibit citizens from purchasing or owning firearms. Supporters of gun freedoms and gun control question everything from the amendment's grammar and word choice to what the authors of the Bill of Rights meant when they wrote it in 1791.

Those who oppose gun control say the Second Amendment clearly defines ownership of guns as a right of every American when it says "the right of the people to keep and bear arms shall not be infringed." Not only does the amendment guarantee citizens the right to have guns, they say, it states that this right shall not be violated. "Man has natural, unalienable rights. Among these are the rights to life, liberty, and property," says historian Benedict D. LaRosa. "If he possesses these rights, then he must also possess a right to defend them. If he has a right to defend them, then he has a right to the means with which to defend them." Those who read the Second Amendment this way see gun control measures of any kind as unconstitutional. "The Founders were so adamant about protecting the right of every individual to keep and bear arms, they prohibited even trespassing upon the fringes or outer edges of that right,"[13] LaRosa says.

If the second half of the amendment is read literally by gun rights supporters, the first half is what gun control activists focus on. They read the phrase "a well-regulated militia being necessary to the security of a free state" to mean that the right of the

The Second Amendment, granting Americans the right to keep and bear arms, was written in 1791, and its interpretation has been hotly debated ever since.

The 2nd Amendment

still stands

people to keep and bear arms is only for the purpose of establishing a well-regulated militia. "Leading up to the adoption of the Constitution and the Bill of Rights, no law in any of the states, colonies, or territories had used the phrase 'bear arms' in anything but a military sense," says Second Amendment researcher Patrick J. Charles. "The use of the phrase 'bear arms' was distinctively limited to use in each of the colonies' militia laws."[14] A militia, in the late 1700s, was an army made up of citizens rather than a professional army of paid soldiers. In 1791 Americans believed very strongly in a militia, which had helped them win independence from Britain, but in the twenty-first century, a militia is no longer the main way the United States protects itself. If the Second Amendment only means citizens can be armed as part of a regulated militia, this could outdate the entire amendment.

By questioning whether the Second Amendment is necessary in modern times, however, advocates of gun control may threaten the entire Bill of Rights, say opponents. If the government decides that the right to keep and bear arms no longer applies to U.S. citizens on the grounds that it was based on the country's needs in the eighteenth century, then any of the Bill of Rights' first ten freedoms, all passed the same year as the Second Amendment, might someday be questioned as no longer being necessary in an evolving nation. "As long as the government as a whole and people in the government feel that the Second Amendment can be rendered meaningless and ignored, no aspect of the Constitution can be considered sacrosanct [sacred],"[15] says gun rights researcher and author Theodore L. Johnson.

The Second Amendment in Court

Declaring the Second Amendment no longer applicable could be disastrous for existing gun laws in the United States, since the law has been used to help the Supreme Court uphold its decisions about gun rights for nearly 150 years. The court made its first decision about the Second Amendment in 1876 when it ruled that the Constitution did not grant the right to keep and bear arms—but it said the Constitution did not grant the First Amendment rights to free speech and religion, either. These were fundamental human rights people already had before the Constitution was ever written, the ruling stated, and the federal government did not have the power to give people these freedoms *or* to take them away. The court thus upheld the idea that Americans could rightly possess and use firearms the same as they could speak freely and practice their chosen religion.

In 1939 the Supreme Court heard another case about the right to keep and bear arms. This case was about whether the Second Amendment applied to any kind of gun a citizen might want to possess. Through the National Firearms Act of 1934, Congress put limits on the right to own certain kinds of weapons—in particular, machine gun–style weapons popular among the brutal street gangs of the 1920s and 1930s. Shortly after the National Firearms Act was passed, a man named Jack Miller was charged with owning a newly regulated assault weapon. Miller argued that the National Firearms Act violated the Second Amendment. In *United States v. Miller*, The Supreme Court decided that Miller or any other American citizen could own one of the banned weapons only if he or she could prove the weapon was specifically for use in the regulated militia that the Second Amendment mentioned.

The 1939 ruling did not state that citizens could never own a restricted or banned weapon but that they would have to justify their purpose for owning one. The court's decision was taken to mean that the Second Amendment supported the idea of a militia more than a particular citizen's right to own weapons— which was a highly controversial view. "The *Miller* decision was widely accepted by the federal courts of appeals as evidence of a *rejection* of an individual right to keep and bear arms," says former Supreme Court law clerk Earl E. Pollack. "This consensus was sharply challenged by what became a flood of scholarly articles based on new analysis of the history and purpose of the Second Amendment."[16]

The arguments about the right to keep and bear arms continued into the twenty-first century. In 2008 another landmark case about the Second Amendment landed in the Supreme Court. The city of Washington, D.C., had prohibited its citizens from owning or carrying a handgun since 1976. In

A woman practices at a shooting range. Opponents of gun control claim that if the Second Amendment were overturned, the whole Bill of Rights would be in jeopardy.

2008 the Supreme Court heard a case involving Dick Heller, a security guard for the city. Heller carried a handgun every day for his job but was forced to leave it at work at the end of every shift. City law forbade him to keep a handgun in his own home for self-protection. He sued the city, saying the Second Amendment gave him the right to keep a handgun at home. The Supreme Court ruled in Heller's favor, stating that the Second Amendment does indeed give citizens the right to keep and bear arms and that the city's practice of banning all handguns was unconstitutional. The decision was seen as a major step in favor of gun ownership among Americans.

Legal Limits on Guns

In the *District of Columbia v. Heller* case, the Supreme Court interpreted the Second Amendment as guaranteeing people the right to own firearms, including handguns. This does not mean the court guarantees all citizens the right to own any weapon

The Straw Story

Gun laws in the United States forbid certain people from buying guns, including convicted felons and legal minors. Many criminals get around these laws using what is known as a straw purchase—they enlist someone who will pass the background check to buy guns for them. These stand-in buyers, called straws, are often spouses, friends, or girlfriends or boyfriends. Sometimes the person who wants the gun accompanies the straw into the store, points out the gun he or she wants, and even gives the straw money for the purchase in front of the store clerk. In other cases the criminals who buy the guns are not the ones who use them. Instead, they sell firearms to other criminals for a marked-up price. Those buying and moving the guns are called traffickers, and they supply the so-called black market of the gun trade. As many as 40 percent of guns used in crime are not sold to the criminals who use them but to straw purchasers. This shows that gun control laws, like background checks, are easy for savvy criminals to get around, especially when there are legal sellers willing to overlook signs of straw purchasing.

they choose, however. Assault weapons, generally defined as firearms that can shoot in a semiautomatic or fully automatic mode, have been a continuing subject of the gun control debate. A semiautomatic weapon fires a bullet with each pull of the trigger until all the bullets in the ammunition container (the clip) are shot. An automatic weapon sprays bullets until the shooter releases the trigger or the gun runs out of ammunition. Gun control laws have banned such assault weapons over the years. In 1994 Congress also banned any gun with certain features that gave it an assault purpose, such as a folding stock (the handle or shoulder piece to which the barrel of the gun attaches), a pistol grip that allows users to hold a rifle like a handgun, or a flash suppressor (a device that attaches to the end of a gun barrel to hide the sudden burst of flame emitted when the gun is fired).

People who seek guns for legal reasons like hunting or self-defense are unlikely to need either a flash suppressor or a fully automatic weapon. "What blessed use is there for one of these assault weapons?" asks former Pennsylvania governor Ed Rendell, a supporter of the bans. "What American needs an assault weapon to protect themselves?"[17]

On the other hand, bans on assault-style weapons may unfairly assume their owners plan to use them for crime. Not until a person has committed a crime can he or she be considered a criminal, and simply owning a particular weapon does not mean a person will use it against others. Many gun rights defenders therefore interpret these gun control efforts as a limit on their constitutional freedoms. "'Who needs an assault weapon?' is an illegitimate question," says the National Rifle Association. "In a free society, the burden of proof is not upon those who wish to exercise rights, it is upon those who wish to restrict rights."[18] Furthermore, guns that are classified as military-style assault weapons make up a very small percentage of all weapons used in actual crimes—just 1 to 2 percent, according to the U.S. Bureau of Justice Statistics. The practice of banning assault weapons, therefore, has little effect on curbing crimes committed with guns, which makes it hard to justify such laws in the first place.

Handguns as Targets

The type of guns used in the vast majority of gun-related crimes in the United States are not assault-style weapons at all but handguns, firearms that can be held, carried, and fired using only one hand, such as a pistol or revolver. A handgun's small size makes it easy to carry, hide under clothing, or store in a home or vehicle. In part because they are so portable, handguns are by far the most common type of firearm used by criminals in America. According to a report by the Bureau of Justice Statistics in 2006, about 68 percent of murders in the United States are committed with firearms, and handguns are used in murders two to three times as often as any other kind of gun. Regulating handguns more strictly, therefore, would arguably have a far larger effect on crime than regulating assault weapons.

Gun rights activists, however, use the same argument against banning handguns as they do against banning assault weapons—just because someone owns a handgun does not mean he or she is going to use it to commit a crime. "Anti-gun people persist in believing that their neighbors and co-workers will become mass murderers if allowed to own firearms," says psychiatrist and gun rights activist Sarah Thompson, but "the anti-gun person who believes that malicious shootings by ordinary gun owners are likely to occur is not in touch with reality."[19] Handguns appeal to noncriminals for many of the same reasons they appeal to criminals—they are smaller, more lightweight, easier to store, and easier to load and fire than long guns like rifles and shotguns. This makes them well suited for self-defense. Criminals may use handguns more than any other type of weapon, but prohibiting the weapons would prevent law-abiding citizens from owning this popular type of gun as well.

According to the Bureau of Justice Statistics, about 68 percent of murders in the United States in 2006 were committed with firearms—handguns accounting for two to three times as many as any other kind of gun.

Portable Guns

Much of the gun control issue has centered on regulating what types of guns are or should be available to citizens, such as handguns or assault weapons. Other efforts to control gun violence have to do with where and how people are allowed to use and store their firearms. A gun kept at home is unlikely to be used for crime, but guns carried outside of one's home are far more likely to be fired, with potentially deadly consequences. Whether people should have a right to carry a firearm with them when they leave their home—specifically, a portable handgun that is easy to conceal—is another debated aspect of gun control.

DANGER AT HOME

"The risk does not come from homicidal maniacs or muggers or rapists. The risk comes from *people using their own guns to shoot themselves or their family members.*" —Human behavior columnist Shankar Vedantam

Shankar Vedantam. *The Hidden Brain: How Our Unconscious Minds Elect Presidents, Control Markets, Wage Wars, and Save Our Lives.* New York: Spiegel & Grau, 2010, p. 235.

U.S. citizens, lawmakers, and government officials have debated concealed-carry policies for about two centuries. The Wild West during the 1800s provided examples of the dangers of armed citizens in the streets. Criminals carried handguns, and therefore, many law-abiding citizens felt they were safer if they did, too. If someone drew a weapon, several bystanders were likely to pull out their own guns. Such tense situations sometimes led to shootouts, and any innocent bystander could be caught in the crossfire. Citizens of the Wild West quickly took steps to stop lawless gun shooting. "Even in the most violence-prone western towns, gunplay and lawlessness were only briefly tolerated,"[20] says political science professor Robert J. Spitzer.

Carrying concealed weapons is as controversial today as it was back then—and for the same reasons. Criminals can and do hide handguns in their clothing and carry them wherever they go, and citizens who are not criminal minded often feel safer if they carry a handgun, too. If many people walking around a city or town are armed, any argument or dispute could potentially lead to drawn weapons and deadly shootings. Innocent bystanders can be caught in the crossfire and injured or killed. The violence among modern street gangs exemplifies what can happen when people walk around armed—gang members get into disputes and shoot at each other, and all too often their bullets go astray and wound or kill innocent people.

Many gun control activists favor laws that do not forbid people to *own* guns but that do forbid them to *carry* a gun in public places, especially if the gun is concealed beneath clothing or in a backpack or other type of handbag so that it is not readily visible to others. Nevertheless, as of 2012 Illinois was the only state that completely forbade carrying a loaded gun in public. All other states have laws allowing at least some citizens to carry loaded weapons, although most states require a person to have a special license or permit in order to carry a gun in public, and this permit dictates whether the gun must be visible or can be concealed. To receive such a permit, a person typically must pass classes to prove he or she is knowledgeable about gun safety and knows how to use a gun properly. Most states' permits also require a criminal background check of the applicant, and the permit usually only applies in the state in which it was issued. States that allow visible (open) gun carrying by citizens often limit the places people can go with a visible weapon, in part because the sight of a gun can be intimidating to fellow citizens or could confuse police officers should a crime occur. States that offer concealed-carry permits often restrict the places where a citizen can have a gun as well. For example, weapons may be forbidden in state or federal buildings and on school campuses.

Even with these restrictions on carried weapons, gun control activists say cities and towns are more dangerous if people can walk around armed. On the other hand, say gun rights activists, criminals such as gang members pay no attention to laws and will not hesitate to carry hidden guns and pull them out to use them in public places, so law-abiding citizens should be able to carry a gun of their own for self-defense if they choose. "The problem with concealed weapons is that criminals carry them

Hidden Guns

Permits to carry guns are among the most contested aspects of gun control. States pass their own legislation to allow or deny citizens the right to carry any loaded firearm in public—whether visible or hidden from view. States that allow visible (open) and/or concealed gun carrying choose between "may issue" and "shall issue" policies. "May issue" means permits are dispensed case by case at the state's discretion. "Shall issue" means the state grants a permit to any applicant who meets basic requirements such as minimum age. All but six states allowed some form of open carrying as of 2012. Concealed carrying was rare in the 1980s, when only four states were "shall issue" states and many prohibited concealed carrying altogether, but the practice has swept like a fad through the nation since then. As of 2012, eight states were "may issue," thirty-seven were "shall issue," and four others required no permit and placed no restrictions at all on concealed carrying. Only Illinois and the District of Columbia (Washington, D.C.) completely prohibited the carrying of concealed firearms as of 2012. Ironically, D.C., known for the nation's strictest gun control laws, also has the nation's highest gun-related death rate, five times higher than the national average. Utah, with some of the nation's most lenient right-to-carry laws, has the lowest death rate due to guns.

Illinois gun owners in 2011 protest their state's lack of a concealed carry law—the only state without such a law.

and use them against their victims," says economist Fred E. Foldvary. "But criminals are already outside the law, so they carry the weapon law or no law. Concealed weapon permit holders are seldom the perpetrators of violent crimes."[21] Whether law-abiding U.S. citizens should be allowed to carry loaded firearms, either concealed or visible, is another ongoing part of the gun controversy.

Check and Wait

Aside from outlawing guns completely or restricting where they can be carried, gun control efforts have included measures that focus on purchases of new guns. Background checks, for example, have been required since 1968 to purchase a firearm and are designed to keep guns out of the hands of people who are likely to use them in a crime or to be involved in a gun-related accident. Gun sellers have access to computer databases that allow them to conduct background checks quickly, often within minutes, which is a small inconvenience for a lawful gun buyer. Arguably, no one would complain about a background check except people who have criminal or mental-health records they wish to hide from the gun seller, so this is touted as a common-sense gun control measure.

SAVAGE HUMANS

"Those who believe in a strong activist government generally do so because they fear the potential savagery of human social life. They just don't seem to want, with gun control, to allow the *individual* to do anything about it."—Brian Doherty, senior editor, *Reason* magazine

Brian Doherty. "How the Second Amendment Was Restored." *Reason*, December 2008. http://reason.com/archives/2008/11/18/how-the-second-amendment-was-r/singlepage.

Waiting periods are slightly more controversial. A waiting period requires a certain amount of time—usually a few days to a week—to pass after a gun purchase before the buyer can take the weapon out of the store. Waiting periods were once required

Some states require a waiting period—usually a few days to a week—after a gun purchase before the buyer can take the weapon out of the store. Such requirements have proved controversial.

by all gun sellers in the country, in part because it took several days to conduct a criminal background check on a prospective gun buyer. The federal law requiring waiting periods expired in 1999 because background checks can now be done in moments by computers, but many states have reinstituted waiting periods for the purchase of all or just certain kinds of guns. Crime research shows that people who buy a gun specifically to hurt someone use it soon after buying it. A waiting period gives buyers time to cool off and reconsider their plan.

Although some gun rights supporters oppose waiting periods on the basis that they believe any gun control measure abuses their rights, gun control advocates believe that for people such as hunters or recreational shooters who do not want a gun for any criminal purpose, minor controls like waiting periods and background checks are not an infringement on lifestyle or rights. "All we really want are sensible restrictions based on public safety and common sense," says *New York*

Times editorial-page editor Andrew Rosenthal. "Go ahead, buy a gun. Use it to hunt, for target practice, in a collection, or in case you need to defend your home. Just register it and submit to a background check."[22]

Ammunition Wars

Still other regulations on firearms have nothing to do with waiting periods or background checks for guns but instead apply to bullets. Controlling ammunition by limiting the type and quantity of bullets a person can purchase or own has long been seen as a way to curb the potential danger of guns. A typical person who owns a handgun for self-defense should not anticipate needing hundreds of bullets on hand to fend off an intruder, whereas

In an effort to curb gun violence, seven states have proposed taxes on ammunition.

someone with criminal intentions may stock up on pistol bullets before going on a shooting spree. Restricting or outlawing such ammunition is another approach to gun control.

Because bullets themselves do not require background checks and are widely available, it is difficult to keep track of how many bullets one person buys and possesses and therefore to regulate guns this way. In 2012 Illinois joined six other states—California, Louisiana, Massachusetts, New Jersey, Oklahoma, and Pennsylvania—that have proposed taxes on gun ammunition as a way to curb problems with gun violence. If bullets were extremely expensive, people would be less inclined to have an arsenal. They would instead be likely to buy and keep only the minimal ammunition they needed for self-protection or hunting.

Such tax proposals have met with staunch opposition that has prevented them from passing. Many gun supporters see such regulations and taxes on bullets as a sneaky way for gun control activists to get around the Second Amendment. "Some have suggested banning the further manufacture of ammunition instead of guns,"[23] says criminologist Gary Kleck. A gun with no bullets, gun activists reason, is as useless as having no gun at all, so ammunition regulation is really a form of gun control. Even raising the price of ammunition through reduced availability or taxes is seen as unfair to many people in America. Wealthy citizens would still be able to afford bullets even if high taxes were placed on them, whereas people who make less money would not have the same access to ammunition and any benefits firearms might provide to the rich. Regulating ammunition through laws or taxes remains a highly controversial aspect of gun control.

Legal Battles March On

As arguments over ammunition affordability show, proposed regulations on firearms are not just about guns but are linked to beliefs about social classes, the causes and consequences of crime, and the very meaning of the Constitution. There are no easy answers in the gun control debate, but because gun ownership is seen as a life-and-death topic, it is one of the most emotionally charged issues in the United States today. Ongoing arguments for and against it create complex dilemmas. Meanwhile, activists on both sides tend to misrepresent facts or skew statistics to suit their own arguments. Fully understanding the issue involves a careful consideration of the concerns and opinions of those who favor stricter gun control and those who oppose it, and they both argue passionately for their views.

ARGUMENTS IN FAVOR OF GUN CONTROL

Guns result in the death of thirty thousand people on average every year in the United States via murder, suicide, and accidents. Another one hundred thousand people per year are wounded by gunfire. Guns were the third leading cause of injury-related death in the United States in 2009; among accidental deaths only automobile accidents and poisoning killed more people. More American civilians die from fatal gunshots every seven days than the number of American soldiers killed in the line of duty in the first seven years of the U.S.-Iraq war, according to the Law Center to Prevent Gun Violence. Gunshots kill more American civilians every two years than the fifty-eight thousand who died between 1955 and 1975 during the Vietnam War. In a 2003 study, the National Institutes of Health found that overall homicide rates involving firearms were 19.5 percent higher in the United States than in twenty-three other countries with similar populations and per-person income. Of the total gun-related murders reported by all twenty-four countries combined, 80 percent of them happened in the United States.

The United States also has the world's highest concentration of gun ownership. There are about 300 million guns in the United States, a country with a population of 308 million people. About half of these people exercise their constitutional right to possess firearms—a right that is more lenient in the United States than in almost any other country in the world. According to a 2007 study by the Graduate Institute of International Studies in Geneva, Switzerland, Americans purchase about 56 percent of all new guns manufactured in the world each year, even though they account for only about 4.5 percent of the world's

The United States has the world's highest concentration of gun ownership, with nearly 300 million guns for a population of 308 million people.

total population. Statistically, the United States sees the most gun violence of any country in the world and also has the highest gun ownership per capita. These statistics support arguments that the United States would be safer if its government regulated guns more strictly.

Guns Make Murder Easier

Murder is the biggest worry associated with guns. Homicides are much more common in the United States than in other nations with a comparable standard of living, such as Canada, Japan, and the countries of Europe. Approximately 5 Americans per 100,000 are murdered each year, according to the United Nations International Homicide Statistics, far higher than the reported rates of about 1.5 per 100,000 in England and Canada and 0.5 per 100,000 in Japan. Of the Americans who lose their lives to homicide each year, 68 percent are killed with guns.

Firearms by themselves do not hurt anybody, but in the hands of someone who intends to injure or kill, guns are very effective tools for the job. They are designed to put a bullet through a living target with deadly force. Gunshots are immediate—the bullet reaches the victim before he or she even hears the sound of the shot, leaving no time to duck or seek cover. Unlike weapons such as knives or clubs, which require an attacker to approach the victim, guns can be fired from a long distance away, preventing a victim from having any chance at fending off or outrunning an assailant. The long-distance killing ability of a gun can make it difficult for shooters to be caught, as well, since victims and witnesses may not immediately know even the direction the bullet came from. It is often easy for a shooter to get away unseen and hard for police to identify and track down the person.

PROTECT ME NOT

"I believe that when you tell me that you're going to protect the neighborhood that I live in, I don't want you to have a gun."— Comedian and actor Bill Cosby

Quoted in Dylan Stableford. "Bill Cosby on George Zimmerman: Guns, Not Race, Real Issue in Trayvon Martin Case." *The Cutline* (blog), Yahoo! News, April 15, 2012. http://news.yahoo.com/blogs/cutline/cosby-george-zimmerman-guns-not-race-real -issue-184628189.html.

Guns are designed to kill people, not just hurt them, but many shooters' lack of accuracy means that only one in three gunshot victims dies from his or her wounds. Twice the number of people killed by guns live through being shot, and a bullet wound may affect them for life. Gunshot wounds can permanently impair a victim, especially if the brain or spinal cord is injured. A victim may live through a shooting but have lifelong disabilities. Many shooting victims are innocent bystanders and are not even the person at whom the shooter was aiming. Some of them are children. Gun control activists call for stronger policies to end these tragedies. "However 'difficult' it is for a politician to stand up to the gun lobby, it is far more difficult for a parent to bury a child, for a sister to bury a brother,"[24] says Dennis Henigan, acting president of the Brady Campaign.

Stand Your Ground

On the evening of February 26, 2012, twenty-eight-year-old George Zimmerman was volunteering for a neighborhood watch in Sanford, Florida, when he saw seventeen-year-old Trayvon Martin walking in the rain. Zimmerman called 9-1-1 and said that the African American teen looked suspicious. Shortly after seven o'clock, Zimmerman shot and killed Martin. He later told police he had acted in self-defense. Martin had been walking home from a convenience store and carried only a bag of candy and a bottle of iced tea. The case became one of the most high-profile shootings of the year. It highlighted potential racial tensions (many people believed Zimmerman, a Hispanic, had pro-filed a black teenager), but it also put a spotlight on the controversy of gun rights. Specifically, the case dealt with Florida's Stand Your Ground law, which states that people can use deadly force, such as shooting someone to protect themselves or their property, without first making every possible effort to retreat or get away. Zimmerman reported that Martin had attacked him. Even if that were the case, people questioned whether Zimmerman needed to shoot the teen to death. Stand Your Ground laws have been heavily criticized for encouraging people to solve confrontations with violence instead of considering other options like backing away or waiting for police to arrive.

The legal defense of George Zimmerman, center, charged in the shooting death of seventeen-year-old Trayvon Martin, will be centered around Florida's controversial Stand Your Ground law.

Despite the already high toll of gun-caused death and injury and the calls of gun control activists to temper deadly firearms, gun manufacturers often sell weapons with improvements or accessories that make them even more lethal. Laser sights, for example, cast a laser beam that shows up as a red dot at the precise point where the bullet will hit, making it far less likely that a bullet will miss its victim. Silencing devices can be screwed onto the barrel of some guns to muffle the loud sound characteristic of a gunshot, making it possible to shoot without sending bystanders scattering or alerting witnesses. Ammunition cartridges, especially popular for handguns, make it possible to shoot multiple bullets before needing to stop and reload the gun, so an assailant can keep shooting rapidly, increasing the chances that at least one bullet will connect with the victim.

Inventions like these are designed to give the person holding the gun even more advantages. Journalist Eric Larson says a "conspiracy of gun dealers" makes "ever more powerful guns, and laser sights, silencer-ready barrels, folding stocks, exploding bullets . . . all too easy to come by, and virtually assures their eventual use in the bedrooms, alleys and school yards of America."[25] Gun control supporters believe the government has an obligation to regulate how widespread and how deadly guns are allowed to become.

Guns and Suicide

Even without laser sights or other accessories, guns make ideal murder weapons. Of the thirty thousand gun-related deaths each year in the United States, however, slightly more than half of them are not murders but suicides. According to the nonprofit research organization Suicide.org, more suicides in the United States are committed using guns—52 percent—than all other suicide methods combined. A gun is a very efficient suicide tool in that its effects are instantaneous. Having a loaded gun accessible in the home is considered a significant risk factor for suicide by firearm. The presence of the gun does not make a person want to commit suicide, but a person with suicidal thoughts who knows the gun is there may make a rash decision to use it. Other methods of suicide, such as jumping

Fifty-two percent of suicides in the United States are committed using guns.

off a high place or obtaining and consuming a lethal dose of pills, take at least a few moments of time and planning that allow the person to consider what he or she is about to do and perhaps seek help. A gun that is readily available at home requires no planning and is an instantaneous and usually successful way to end one's life.

Suicide by gunfire is one of the tragedies gun control activists seek to prevent. According to social worker Alan Schwartz:

> Suicide attempts are viewed as a desperate call for help among those who are depressed or mentally ill with a psychotic illness. . . . Those who succeed in using drugs to attempt suicide are successful only 3% of the time. By contrast, more than 90% of all suicide attempts by use of firearms are successful. The bottom line is that anyone using a gun to commit suicide is not likely to have their call for help heard and responded to before [it is] too late.[26]

Gun control advocates use the gun-associated risk of suicide as further evidence that the nation needs more laws to discourage people from having loaded guns in their home.

Accidental Death by Gunfire

Having a loaded gun accessible at home is dangerous if a member of one's family is suicidal, but gun ownership poses another serious danger, especially in a household with children. About six hundred people in the United States die from accidental gunshot wounds each year, according to the Centers for Disease Control and Prevention (CDC), and anywhere from one-sixth to one-third of them are children. Another 15,500 people are injured from accidental gunshots.

Guns are a widespread and often glorified image in American culture, with movies, television shows, and even cartoons showing guns frequently. Children who see such shows recognize what a gun looks like, how it is held, and what it is used for. Toy weapons like squirt guns and cap guns encourage children to practice aiming and shooting at things and people. If children who have played with guns or seen them on TV come across loaded weapons in their home or the home of a friend or acquaintance, they may believe they know how to handle one and what to do with it, and the consequences can be devastating.

Every year dozens of children and teens in the United States accidentally shoot themselves or someone else with a loaded gun, often one that has been left available by parents who kept the weapon in the home for good intentions like defending the family from intruders. Having a loaded gun accessible in a home with children present is so dangerous that the American Academy of Pediatrics encourages doctors to ask parents about the presence of a gun in their homes just as they ask about other common dangers such as swimming pools. To gun control advocates, requiring people either to give up dangerous guns—especially handguns—altogether or at least to keep them unloaded and locked away when there are children at home is a small and very reasonable price for Americans to pay in exchange for preventing the accidental deaths of children and teens. "Parents often do not realize how easily a child can access a gun that is not locked, and we too often hear about the tragic consequences,"[27] says O. Marion Burton, president of the American Academy of Pediatrics.

The Myth of Gun Ownership and Personal Safety

Gun owners often say they keep a gun in the home for protection from dangerous intruders—and despite the risk of accidental shootings, having children at home only seems to strengthen their commitment to protect themselves and their family with a firearm. According to the Bureau of Justice Statistics and U.S. Census data, the likelihood of having one's home broken into is about 3 in 1,000 (although the risk of home invasion varies widely, depending on where people live). This probability of a home break-in is not considerably higher than the 2.6-in-1,000 probability that a member of a gun-owning household will cause or be a victim of a shooting accident. Keeping a loaded gun around the house is, in many cases, more dangerous to one's family than not having a gun at all, considering that 55 percent of home break-ins that happen when the occupants are home result in no injury at all and only 9 percent result in serious injury to the occupant. Even home break-ins, therefore, may not be as dangerous as home accidents with firearms. Furthermore, there are effective things people can do for self-defense besides owning a gun. Just making sure all doors and windows are closed and locked, for example, would prevent 40 percent of home invasions.

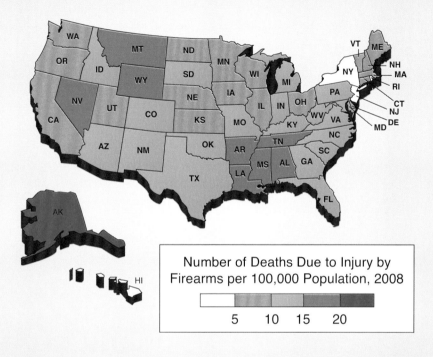

Number of Deaths Due to Injury by Firearms in the United States, 2008

Number of Deaths Due to Injury by Firearms per 100,000 Population, 2008

5   10   15   20

Taken from: Centers for Disease Control and Prevention.

In addition, a gun is not always the most effective choice for fending off an intruder even if a home break-in *does* occur. Gun-safety training and shooting practice are not prerequisites for buying or owning a firearm, and a gun in the hands of an in-experienced user can actually pose a more serious threat to one's family than being unarmed. A bullet passes readily through walls, so a gun fired wildly in the direction of an intruder might miss its target but hit someone in another room. Also, about 12 percent of home intruders are armed themselves. If the home-owner draws a weapon and starts shooting, an armed intruder is likely to return fire and may be much more accurate than the inexperienced homeowner. An unarmed home intruder could

Keeping a loaded gun in the house is more dangerous to one's family than not having a gun at all, according to the Bureau of Justice Statistics.

also manage to wrest a gun away and turn the homeowner's own weapon on him or her. As gun control supporters point out, it can be more dangerous to have a gun in one's home than not to have one at all. Laws prohibiting having weapons at home might actually save lives.

Guns Have No Place in Public Spaces

Although suicides and accidental deaths due to guns are serious problems, most gun control activists are more concerned with what can happen when guns leave people's homes and are carried around in public. Gun owners often wish to carry their weapons in public places for the same reason they want to have loaded guns at home—they want to be able to defend themselves if threatened. However, gun control advocates give some of the same arguments against citizens' carrying loaded guns as they do about having guns at home. Not everyone who carries a gun knows a lot about gun safety or has practiced with the weapon. An inexperienced shooter might fire in a panic and accidentally hit an innocent person standing nearby. A criminal attacker could also take the gun away from an inexperienced victim and use it on the victim or on bystanders. According to a 2009 study published in the *American Journal of Public Health*, a crime victim who carries a gun is 4.5 times more likely to be shot during an assault than a victim who does not carry a gun.

CRIMINAL ELEMENT

"They (gun supporters) believe we need to shift attention to criminals, focus on the criminal, and they absolutely don't see the fact that the people who are committing most of the shootings and murders are not criminals until that moment."—Former Colorado state senator Pat Pascoe

Quoted in Deborah Homsher. *Women & Guns: Politics and the Culture of Firearms in America.* Expanded ed. Armonk, NY: Sharpe, 2002, p. 122.

Thirty-five of the forty-nine states that allow citizens to carry guns require them to go through a permitting process that generally includes training in gun safety and how to handle one's weapon. As of 2012 four states had no such demands, nor do they even require a permit to carry a concealed weapon— Alaska, Arizona, Wyoming, and Vermont. In these states almost anyone over age eighteen could be carrying a loaded weapon legally, even if they have received no training on how to use it safely. Even in states where permits are required to carry a gun outside the home, gun toters with only very basic knowledge or experience with the weapon may be overly confident about their ability to use it.

Increasing the number of guns on the streets also increases the chance of accidents or the likelihood that a dispute over something trivial, such as a drunken argument in a bar or a road rage incident, could turn into a deadly shootout. Loose restrictions on gun ownership also make it easier for people with mental illnesses or simply murderous intentions to get their hands on weapons they can use to injure and kill many unsuspecting people in crowded areas in a matter of moments. Such tragedies happen every year in places like schools, shopping malls, restaurants, parking lots, and movie theaters. Gun control activists disagree that armed bystanders could effectively halt such mass public shootings by firing at the shooter, which is one argument gun rights supporters often make. "The prospect of facing armed opposition hardly dissuades mass murderers . . . who are determined to pursue their vengeful plan," says criminology professor James Alan Fox. "In fact, many mass killers fully expect to die in battle; some even taking their own life."[28]

Gun control activists call for federal and state government to put more limits on who should be able to walk around with a loaded firearm concealed in a purse, backpack, or beneath their clothing. Even though guns are generally banned in schools and other public or government buildings, gun control activists say the people of the United States have a right to go out to dinner, take a walk, see a movie, or do anything else without worrying about strangers carrying loaded guns on streets and sidewalks. Even more troubling for gun control supporters are states that allow citizens to *openly* carry weapons—to have guns that are visible instead of concealed beneath clothing. "There is a universal concern that this will lead to more confrontations with our citizens," says Norman McNickle, president of the Association of Police Chiefs in Oklahoma, where the state government was considering passing an open-carry law in 2012. "How [do] the first arriving officers know who the good guys are and who the bad guys are? It makes their job exponentially harder."[29]

Almost two in three Americans in a 2005 Gallup poll said they would feel less safe in a public place if they knew nonpolice civilians were permitted to carry concealed, loaded guns. "Just as opponents of weak concealed carry laws warned, we now know that concealed handgun permit holders are killing people in road rage incidents, arguments over parking spaces, and domestic disputes," says Kristen Rand, legal policy director of the Violence Policy Center. "The incidents we document graphically demonstrate how the presence of a handgun escalates an argument to a homicide."[30]

A Salt Lake City police officer squats next to a shooting victim at a local mall. Loose restrictions on gun ownership are criticized for making it easier for people with mental illnesses to get a gun that they can use to randomly kill people at schools, malls, restaurants, and movie theaters.

Laws that allow people to own and carry guns may lead gun owners to use guns in self-defense in any situation where they feel threatened, even if a response such as walking away or talking through a misunderstanding would be more effective and sensible. There is also concern that some gun owners, believing in their right to form militias and protect themselves from government abuses, might form antigovernment groups and use firepower to threaten or strike out at government officials or agencies whenever they disagree with something the government does. Supporters of stricter gun control laws say it only makes sense that increasing the number of guns on the streets and in the hands of people will increase gun crime and the use of guns in situations that do not call for them, whereas limiting the carrying of guns in public and private places will logically lower the number of shootings around the nation.

Stricter Gun Laws, Not Stricter Gun Punishments

Gun control supporters argue that the high gun crime rate in the United States is evidence that stricter gun laws are needed, not more lenient concealed-carry policies. They compare the United States with nations like Canada and England, where guns are strictly controlled and murders and gun crimes are far less frequent. "Gun violence in the U.S. is an epidemic," says Adam Cohen of Yale Law School. "American gun-ownership rates are the highest in the world, with a remarkable 88 guns per 100 people." Cohen says gun rights activists "should lighten up . . . and show the nation that gun owners care not only about their own rights but also about the rights of innocent victims of gun violence."[31]

People who oppose gun control often claim that the United States needs stricter punishment for criminals, not stricter laws to keep guns away from law-abiding citizens. But since even more gun deaths result from suicides and accidents than criminal activities, gun control supporters insist that more gun laws and tighter controls *are* needed to keep American citizens safe. Also, stricter punishments for gun-related crimes have not, so far, proved to deter criminals from committing the crimes in the first place. "The question most offenders are asking is, am I going to get caught?" says crime statistics researcher Don Weatherburn. "They're not sitting down and thinking, well if I am caught will I go to jail and if I do how long will I go for?"[32] Gun control supporters say keeping guns out of the hands of criminals in the

A Million Moms

On Mother's Day 2000, three-quarters of a million people gathered at the National Mall in Washington, D.C. They arrived by busload from every state in the nation to take part in history's largest demonstration for stricter gun laws. Actresses Rosie O'Donnell and Susan Sarandon and singer Melissa Etheridge were among the celebrities who joined in the march. An additional quarter of a million demonstrators gathered in cities across the nation, resulting in a million people—primarily moms—standing up against gun violence. Since the original Million Mom March, chapters supporting the movement have united around the country. They continue the mission of persuading elected officials to pass laws restricting guns. They cite statistics such as the approximately nine hundred thousand Americans who have died from gunshots since the 2000 event. Volunteers continue to form a national network of activists who speak out against gun violence and push for laws that do something about it.

On Mother's Day 2000, three-quarters of a million people gathered on the National Mall to demonstrate against gun violence and for stricter gun control laws.

first place will prevent more gun crimes than punishing criminals after they have already hurt someone.

Gun control activists are often accused of wanting to take away all guns from all citizens, but the majority of their arguments stress modifying existing gun laws to make them stricter in sensible ways, not necessarily banishing guns from the United States altogether. They say, for example, that there is little logical reason to oppose policies like waiting periods between buying a gun and taking it home, except by criminals or suicidal individuals who want to use their new purchase for a deadly purpose right away. "It's hard to understand why a person would need a gun immediately," says Richard Durbin, a senator from Illinois who supported the Brady Act's gun control measures throughout the 1990s. "Bringing back the waiting period isn't

Firing into a Crowd

Mass shootings are among the most pressing issues in the gun control debate. They involve people who fire guns into a crowd, causing injuries and deaths. In a 1999 massacre at Colorado's Columbine High School, two high school seniors opened fire on their classmates and teachers, killing thirteen people and injuring twenty-four. Their violence shocked the nation, but unfortunately, similar school shootings have occurred in the years since. In 2007 a student at Virginia Polytechnic Institute and State University shot and killed thirty-two classmates and wounded seventeen in a massacre even deadlier than Columbine.

Mass shootings occur in many venues, not just in schools. In July 2012 a gunman shot and killed twelve people and injured fifty-eight at a Colorado movie theater. He fired aimlessly at complete strangers; some bullets passed through walls to hit unsuspecting moviegoers who were not even in the shooter's line of sight.

Such horrific incidents show what can happen when people with murderous intentions obtain guns. Even if all guns were outlawed, angry or mentally unstable people might find ways to cause injury and death, such as bombing buildings. Nevertheless, mass shootings and their tragic death tolls force society to ask itself what price it is willing to pay for the right to keep and bear arms.

about more government, it's about fewer gun crime victims."[33] Gun control activists argue that restrictions on guns, especially assault weapons and the ammunition for them, would only hinder criminals, not law-abiding citizens who have no intention of assaulting anyone.

The goal of gun control is a safer America, an ideal its supporters say will be best achieved by reducing the number of deadly firearms in the nation and making it more difficult to obtain one. They believe that fewer guns in the hands of fewer people will logically translate to less gun crime. "Much of the resistance to common-sense changes to our gun laws is meant to shut us down and shut us up," says Sarah Brady, cofounder of the Brady Campaign to Prevent Gun Violence. "It is meant to allow the guys with the guns—instead of ordinary Americans like us with the ideas . . . to make the rules."[34] To supporters of increased gun control in America, defending citizens from injuries and deaths caused by guns matters more than defending the centuries-old rules that allow people to have and carry them.

CHAPTER 4

ARGUMENTS IN FAVOR OF GUN RIGHTS

The United States holds personal freedom and the equality of its people as its most basic and important ideals, something advocates of gun rights and gun control both agree on. Unlike gun control advocates, however, gun rights lobbyists believe firepower is one way to ensure that all people are equal. They say the authors of the U.S. Constitution and the Bill of Rights believed in an armed citizenry so much that they wrote it into law. Armed citizens cannot be easily overpowered by armed soldiers or police forces, whereas unarmed citizens can be. The threat of a corrupt government is real; a government can use violence and arsenals of weapons to control its people, and this has happened in countries like Iraq under former military dictator Saddam Hussein and Burma under former military dictator Than Shwe.

The possibility that the United States could someday turn into such a so-called police state is a main reason gun rights supporters cling tightly to their right to own firearms. During the American Revolution, the newly formed United States rebelled against England. Armed men formed militias in the absence of any organized national army, and their guerrilla-style warfare eventually exhausted the more organized British military and earned independence for the United States. Most supporters of gun rights believe that allowing citizens to own guns is essential to a free nation because it guarantees that a government will never easily be able to subdue its own citizens, no matter how powerful an organized national army may be. Many gun owners feel it is the public's responsibility to own guns as a safeguard against potential government oppression.

Supporters of gun ownership also believe guns equalize individual citizens. Those who may be physically smaller or weaker than a potential attacker have a much better chance at protecting themselves if they have a gun than if they face the assailant empty-handed. If guns did not exist, attacks would still happen, and physically strong assailants—who deliberately choose smaller, weaker victims—would win most of the time. The fundamental right of all Americans to defend themselves equally is another chief reason gun rights supporters give for their views. They argue that achieving the goal of equal rights for all citizens in the United States requires fewer restrictions on gun ownership, not more.

Supporters of gun rights believe guns make all citizens—even the physically smaller or weaker—equally able to defend themselves.

Crime Cannot Be Blamed on Guns

Gun rights activists acknowledge that crime in the United States is worse than in other countries with a similar standard of living, but they do not see this as proof that if there were fewer guns in America there would be less crime. The rates of *all* violent crime are higher in the United States, not just violent crime committed with guns. This is a violent country overall, and guns are just one of the tools Americans use against each other. Supporters of gun rights argue that laws to prohibit guns will not stop crime. They believe it would actually have the opposite effect, increasing guns in the hands of criminals who obtain them illegally while reducing the ability of innocent victims to fight back.

According to the Bureau of Justice Statistics, about 5 million violent crimes occurred in the United States in 2011—including

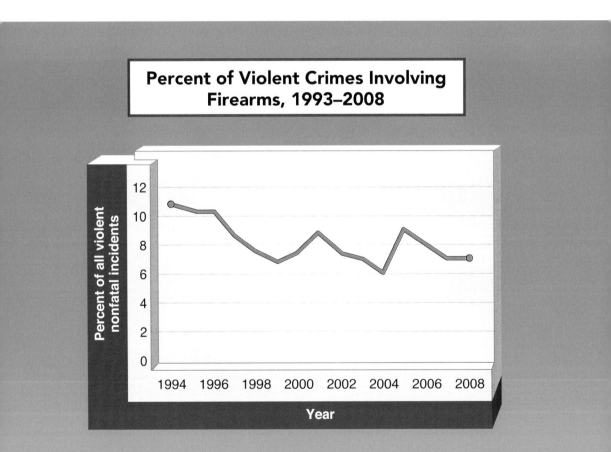

Percent of Violent Crimes Involving Firearms, 1993–2008

Taken from: National Crime Victimization Survey, Bureau of Justice Statistics. bjs.ojp.usdoj.gov/content/glance/percentfirearm.cfm.

murder, rape, sexual assault, robbery, and physical assault—but only 7 percent of those crimes, or about 350,000, were committed with a firearm. Based on these statistics, even if guns vanished from the country altogether, the 4.7 million violent crimes that were not committed with guns would likely have happened anyway. The 7 percent of criminals who did use a gun might even have committed their crimes with another weapon if guns were outlawed. Gun lobbyists point out that guns do not create criminals or cause crime. A gun is simply a device used to commit a crime, the same as some criminals might use an ax or a baseball bat. "These are not death blasters from space!" says Tom Palmer, a plaintiff in the 2008 *District of Columbia v. Heller* Supreme Court case about the Second Amendment. "These are tools. Dangerous tools, like a car, a truck, or a knife are dangerous tools."[35]

Defending Self-Defenders

Although guns are dangerous when used to commit crimes, they are also used in self-defense to stop crimes from happening. Statistics on the number of times guns are used for self-defense in the nation each year are debatable, since the definition of self-defense can range from showing a gun to a potential attacker to actually shooting or shooting at him or her. Police reports are not always filed for incidents where no shots are fired, so polling gun owners is the way most of these statistics are obtained. Based on which researcher or organization conducts the poll and on which methods are used, the number of reported defensive gun uses ranges from 100,000 to more than 2 million incidents every year. The true number likely falls somewhere in between, but even at the very lowest estimate, guns prevent at least 100,000 attacks, murders, robberies, and other crimes yearly. In other words, every year a group of Americans numerous enough to populate a city the size of Berkeley, California, or Cambridge, Massachusetts, uses a gun for self-defense. If the higher end of the estimate is closer to the truth, that city of self-defenders might jump to the size of San Diego, California, or Dallas, Texas. Whether self-defense statistics on the low or the high end are used, gun rights activists contend it is probable that guns used in defense save more lives than the 30,000 lives lost to gunfire each year.

Supporters of gun rights argue that the real crime would be to strip law-abiding citizens of a tool they might use for self-defense. After all, crimes happen suddenly, often in seconds, and usually when the criminal has made sure no one else is nearby who could help the victim. Even if a victim manages to call 911 during the course of a crime, *American Police Beat* magazine reports that in most American cities it takes an average of nine to eleven minutes for officers to respond to a call—usually enough time for the criminal to complete an attack, robbery, murder, or other crime and get away.

Increasingly, people are deciding it is up to them to protect themselves. Gun lobbyists argue that every law-abiding American deserves the choice to own a gun for that purpose. "Outside of criminology circles, relatively few people can reasonably estimate how often people use guns to fend off criminal attacks," say gun use researchers Clayton E. Cramer and David Burnett. "If policymakers are truly interested in harm reduction, they should pause to consider how many crimes—murders, rapes, assaults, robberies—are thwarted each year by ordinary persons with guns."[36] Because researchers are not sure exactly how many people do use guns for self-defense, restricting gun access could put millions of people at greater risk of being victimized and could actually increase the nation's crime rates.

Suicide Is Not Gun Specific

The number of guns used in self-defense is hard to track, but the number of suicides in the United States each year is reliable. More firearm-related deaths in the United States are due to suicide than homicide, a statistic that has led gun control activists to say that having a gun and ammunition in one's home is a risk factor for suicide. Supporters of gun rights, on the other hand, say that merely having a gun in one's home does not make a person suicidal. There is no link between having a loaded weapon and wanting to use it to end one's life. Rather, suicide is a desperate act related to one or more underlying mental or psychological causes. Once a person decides to attempt suicide, there

Stand and Defend

On New Year's Eve 2011, twenty-four-year-old Sarah McKinley was alone with her three-month-old baby in her home in Blanchard, Oklahoma. Her husband had died of cancer less than a week earlier, on Christmas Day. McKinley lived in a rural area far from the nearest neighbors. When two men started pounding on her door, high on prescription pain pills and threatening to break in so they could steal her late husband's medication, McKinley called 911 and asked if a police officer could be sent right away. No officers were close enough to arrive within the twenty-minute duration of her phone call. When one of the men forced his way in, McKinley defended herself and her child by killing the intruder with one blast of a shotgun. He was armed with a knife, and she recognized him as a man who had harassed her before. Cases like these demonstrate why many people think it is worthwhile to own firearms. Without her shotgun, McKinley and her infant would have been at the mercy of two intoxicated, armed intruders, with police too far away to help.

Sarah McKinley and her infant son stand in her rural Oklahoma home, where she shot and killed one of two home invaders in early 2012. Charges were not filed against her.

are many methods for doing so. The fact that many suicidal people choose a gun for this purpose does not mean guns make people suicidal any more than crossing the Golden Gate Bridge (the world's most common site for suicide) makes someone feel compelled to jump off.

Gun rights lobbyists say suicidal people would find ways to die even if all guns in America were to vanish. They point out that the decision to kill oneself is made first, and *then* the method for doing it is decided on. "Because essentially all suicide attempters have many other highly lethal means available to them, the absence of guns would make very little difference as to how many of them would succeed in killing themselves," says criminologist and criminal justice professor Gary Kleck. "Virtually all

Supporters of gun rights say guns do not make people any more suicidal then does crossing the Golden Gate Bridge, the site of many suicides.

would substitute essentially equally lethal methods, hanging or drowning themselves, breathing exhaust fumes, or using some other method if a gun were not available."[37] Gun rights activists believe encouraging people who have suicidal thoughts to seek help would be a better way to cut down on suicides than enforcing stricter gun laws.

IF ONLY THERE WERE GUNS ON CAMPUS

"Speaking for myself, I would give anything if someone on campus, a professor, one of the trained military or guardsman taking classes or another student could have saved my daughter by shooting Cho before he killed our loved ones." —Holly Adams, mother of a victim of the 2007 Virginia Tech massacre

Quoted in Virginia Citizens Defense League. "A VT Victim's Parent Speaks Out AGAINST Gun Control," April 16, 2012. www2.vcdl.org/webapps/vcdl/vadetail .html?RECID=6619361.

The Ruse of Accidental Shootings

Accidental shootings, especially of children, are an even more compelling reason than suicide to argue in favor of gun control. However, supporters of gun rights point out that the number of accidental deaths of children by firearms falls far short of the number one killer: accidental drowning. About ninety children die from gun accidents each year, according to the American Academy of Pediatrics, but the CDC reports that about seven hundred children die each year from accidental drowning. Any accidental death is tragic, especially when it involves a child, but statistically, guns are far from the deadliest danger to American kids. According to economists Steven D. Levitt and Stephen J. Dubner, "In a given year, there is one drowning of a child for every 11,000 residential pools in the United States. . . . Meanwhile, there is 1 child killed by a gun for every 1 million-plus guns. . . . The likelihood of death by pool (1 in 11,000) versus death by gun (1 in 1 million-plus) isn't even close."[38] If saving children's lives is the primary goal, then it might make more sense to ban swimming pools than to ban guns.

Family and colleagues attend the funeral of a U.S. Border Patrol agent who was accidentally shot and killed by fellow agents. Gun opponents claim shooting accidents are a good reason to ban guns, but proponents claim that other dangers, such as drowning, car accidents, and poisonings, far exceed the danger posed by accidental shootings.

Accidental shootings among the adult population occur as well, although these incidents are so infrequent that gun lobbyists say attention should be focused instead on truly common causes of death. In 2009 the CDC reported about six hundred accidental deaths by gunshot, all ages included. The CDC also reported that car accidents killed about forty-four thousand people that year, and accidental poisonings (by adults and children alike) killed about thirty thousand. Falls, choking, and drowning are other leading types of fatal accidents. Together, these five causes of death—car accidents, poisoning, falls, choking, and drowning—account for 83 percent of all accidental deaths in America, according to the National Safety Council, and unintentional shootings are not among them.

Most gun rights lobbyists fully support measures to make guns safer and educate gun owners about safely using and storing their weapons, but they point out that according to the CDC's statistics, gun deaths accounted for only about one-tenth of 1 percent of all accidental deaths in the United States in the first decade of the new millennium. "This does not imply that accidental shootings are not tragic or that we should not try to reduce their number," says political science professor Harry L. Wilson, but he says gun accidents "are not an epidemic"[39] either. The government's resources would be better spent addressing very common dangers like car accidents than passing more restrictive firearm laws to prevent gun accidents.

More Guns Do Not Equal More Crime

Shooting accidents and suicides are common reasons given by people who seek stricter gun control measures, but guns in the hands of criminals are the largest national concern about firearms overall. The main reason gun control advocates give for wanting stricter laws on guns is that they believe fewer guns translate to fewer crimes and more guns translate to more crimes. In the minds of many Americans, guns and crime rates are linked, and the fear of gun-wielding criminals inevitably leads to calls for greater controls to stamp out the scourge of firearms in America.

Actual statistics on gun ownership, however, do not support the idea that more guns in the hands of more people translates to more crime. In fact, the opposite has proved to be true. Since 1994 the number of guns owned by American citizens has risen by 108 million to a total of about 300 million firearms, according to the National Institute of Justice. In 2011 the FBI conducted an all-time high of 16.5 million background checks on people purchasing new weapons. The 36 percent increase in private firearms owned by the U.S. population since the mid-1990s should translate to a surge in crime if gun control activists' logic about gun availability is correct. However, the *Washington Post* reports that crime has been on a steady decline for decades, and 2011 saw a 4 percent decrease in violent crime nationally over 2010, despite record sales of guns. Of the 300 million guns that exist in the United States, about 500,000 are used in crimes each year, according to the National Institute of Justice—or about 0.04 percent. Put another way, 99.96 percent of all guns in the United States in any given year are not used to commit a crime. These statistics suggest that an increase in guns is not linked to an increase in crime and that criminals use only a tiny proportion of America's guns.

The nation's violent crime rate in 2011 was at its lowest point in forty-one years, even as gun ownership reached an all-time high. Criminologists who study crime trends point out that there are many social factors affecting the crime rate, and gun ownership is clearly not the most important one. The concern that guns cause crime has not played out in recent decades—adding more guns to the population has not resulted in a crime boom.

Gun Control Measures Are Moot

Since the overwhelming majority of Americans' firearms are not used for crime, laws forbidding people to keep and bear arms are seen by most gun owners as only punishing law-abiding citizens for the actions of criminals. Furthermore, the gun control measures that do exist likely have little effect on the number of gun-related crimes, since policies like bans on assault-style weapons, background checks, and waiting periods only work for people who follow the law and obtain their weapons through licensed gun traders. Criminals overwhelmingly do not use legal channels to find their weapons in the first place.

The Bureau of Justice Statistics reports that 40 percent of convicted felons who used a gun in the crime that put them in prison said they got the gun from a friend or family member. Another 40 percent said they bought their gun from an unlicensed seller—the so-called black market, an illegal economy where goods are bought and sold to dodge government regulation. The remaining 20 percent of the felons said they bought their weapons at pawn shops or from licensed retailers at stores or gun shows. According to this study, the government gun regulation that already exists does nothing to prevent eight in

The Bureau of Justice Statistics reports that only 20 percent of felons convicted of gun-related crimes said that they had bought their weapons at licensed pawnshops, stores, or gun shows.

ten gun-wielding criminals from getting a gun without a background check, waiting period, or registration requirement. Placing more restrictions on those who seek guns through legal channels, therefore, does little to prevent most criminals from finding a weapon. "Let's be honest," says Jay Wachtel, an agent for the Bureau of Alcohol, Tobacco, Firearms and Explosives. "If someone wants a gun, it's obvious the person will not have difficulty buying a gun, either legally or through the extensive United States black market."[40]

No Such Thing as a Ban on Guns

The fact that at least 40 percent of criminals admit to getting their guns on the black market, which is impossible for the government to regulate, only makes gun rights activists more determined to maintain their own rights to have a firearm. Criminals will find ways to buy, sell, and possess the weapons no matter what laws the government passes, in much the same way people buy, sell, and use illegal drugs despite the national ban on them. Gun rights activists say that control laws make it harder for law-abiding citizens to obtain weapons but that even if a law were passed forbidding any civilian to own a gun, there would still be guns. They would just be in the hands of criminals who do not follow the law anyway. That would make law-abiding citizens unarmed, easy targets.

GUN FEARERS

"Are criminals afraid of a law-abiding citizen with a gun? You bet! . . . I have seen a criminal who was so frightened of an armed, seventy-year-old woman that in his panic to get away, he turned and ran right into a wall."—Philip Van Cleave, former reserve deputy sheriff

Quoted in John R. Lott. *More Guns, Less Crime: Understanding Crime and Gun Control Laws.* 3rd ed. Chicago: University of Chicago Press, 2010, p. 3.

Washington, D.C., is one example of misguided gun control. In 1976 the city passed the strictest gun control laws in the nation. It forbade anyone to own a handgun that was not registered, and it refused to register any new handgun purchased after 1976, effectively banning handguns for most citizens. Long guns—rifles and shotguns—were permitted in one's home if they were registered, but they had to be stored unloaded, disassembled, and separate from ammunition.

If unarming an entire city was a social experiment in the effectiveness of gun control at curbing crime, it failed miserably. In the years after the ban, the city saw no significant reduction in violent crime. In fact, in the 1990s its violent crime rate soared, and it became known as the murder capital of the United States. The gun ban also did nothing to deter other crimes committed with guns in the city, including home robberies. Armed criminals knew law-abiding homeowners were likely to be unarmed—and even if they were armed, penalties for breaking the gun law and defending oneself with an unauthorized weapon were almost as harsh as the penalties for breaking into someone's home in the first place, making people hesitant to use a gun for self-defense.

In effect, gun control gave Washington, D.C., criminals free rein to terrorize their fellow citizens. "Indeed," said Supreme Court Justice Stephen G. Breyer in the 2008 *Heller* court case about handgun ownership in the city, "a comparison with 49 other major cities reveals that the district's homicide rate is actually substantially higher relative to these other cities than it was before the handgun restriction went into place."[41] Gun rights activists argue that gun bans for the law-abiding actually make it easier for criminals to commit crimes.

There Is No Common Sense in Gun Control

The United States on the whole is not on the verge of adopting national anti-gun laws similar to those in Washington, D.C. Instead, the majority of gun control measures are what many people call commonsense restrictions. It seemingly makes sense, for example, to require gun owners to register their weapons with the government. After all, a driver's license is required for a person to legally operate a vehicle, so having similar restrictions on owning a potentially lethal weapon does not seem unreasonable to gun control advocates. Even most gun rights activists agree that some restrictions on gun ownership are justified. Few people, even those who favor gun ownership, would say a child should be able to buy a gun, for example, or that convicted felons should be able to legally purchase a weapon once they get released from prison. Just as most gun control advocates seek reasonable restrictions on gun ownership rather than the complete ban of all guns in America, most gun rights activists are willing to consider certain policies that restrict gun ownership.

Magic Bullets

Gun control activists are pushing for new technology to be added to every handgun in America. Whenever a gun is shot, a firing pin strikes the bullet casing, a shell containing gunpowder and the bullet. A process called microstamping can put a unique mark on the firing pin so it leaves a specific imprint on every bullet fired out of the gun. The technology could make it possible for police to trace bullets back to the precise handgun that fired them—and to the owner of that gun. Microstamping would make it harder for criminals to get away with gun crimes. Gun rights activists resist the idea of microstamping, however, because it would require millions of gun owners to bring their guns to a retrofitting specialist to equip each weapon with a new firing pin. The estimated cost of this is anywhere from a few dollars to two hundred dollars per gun, and those who cannot afford the fees might be ordered to give up their weapons. Furthermore, the microstamp is not always legible on a fired bullet, possibly making the whole process a waste of resources. Microstamping has become yet another controversial issue in the gun control debate.

A bullet casing shows microstamped identification codes. The microstamping technology could make it possible for police to trace bullets back to the handgun that fired them.

Nevertheless, gun lobbyists are often accused of being obstinate in their opposition to gun control. For example, they typically oppose waiting periods between the time a gun is purchased and the time the buyer is allowed to take it home. They point out that waiting periods can in fact harm people who fear for their life and want a gun immediately for self-defense. A woman who has recently left an abusive husband or boyfriend, for example, might fear he will attack her and therefore buys a gun to protect herself. A waiting period could keep her from taking the weapon home for several days, and during that time she might be attacked or even killed by the man. Gun rights advocates cite instances where such situations have occurred to point out that there are reasons to want a gun right away that have nothing to do with wanting to commit a crime. Many gun rights supporters oppose waiting periods as a needless government control that might harm law-abiding gun buyers but do little to avert gun sales to the many criminals who get their guns through channels that require no waiting period anyway.

Guns Are an American Freedom

Gun lobbyists ardently defend their right to keep and bear arms and oppose many suggested measures by the government to infringe on this right. They do not see gun control as having anything but a worsening effect on crime in the United States, and they point out that the overwhelming majority of guns and gun owners are not criminals but law abiding citizens whose guns are never used in a crime, a suicide, or a fatal accident. At best, gun rights supporters perceive any government effort to control firearms as misinterpreting gun statistics and taking away an important American freedom when there is absolutely no proof that doing so will reduce crime (if anything, they say, it could increase crime). At worst, gun lobbyists see gun control as an insidious government effort to control American citizens by removing their ability to stand up for themselves if the government ever does become corrupt and turn on its people.

Supporters of guns and the Second Amendment are typically suspicious of any proposed law that could threaten or diminish gun ownership among the law-abiding people of America. Americans, they say, should have the choice about whether or not to carry a gun, rather than have the government make that choice for them. "Gun advocates favor freedom, choice and self-responsibility," says journalist and reporter John Stossel, a former coanchor of the ABC News program *20/20*. "If someone wishes to be prepared to defend himself, he should be free to do so. No one has the right to deprive others of the means of effective self-defense, like a handgun."[42]

THE GUN CONTROL
BATTLE RAGES ON

People have conducted studies and collected statistics about guns and crime in America for decades, and the more the issue is studied, the more complicated it becomes. Researchers typically have an agenda—they want to show that guns are either bad or good for America, depending on whether they support gun control or gun rights. Those who seek tighter gun restrictions collect data and cite studies about gun violence, accidents, and reckless gun ownership. Those who seek fewer laws regulating gun possession collect data and cite studies about self-defense, gun-related sports, and responsible gun ownership. Even statistics from unbiased studies are often used by both sides of the debate to support their own arguments. For example, a study on the number of people killed by guns each year may be used to argue that guns are deadly and should be banned but also to argue that guns are less deadly than many other things like automobiles and poisonous substances. The gun control battle is largely a war of statistics, and each side positions the numbers in a way that supports its own views about guns.

The media add to the dispute. Every time there is a mass shooting, national media coverage is intense and often lasts for weeks, creating a surge of sympathy and outrage and fueling arguments that guns should be banned. Conversely, in order to rally more support for guns, media outlets such as outdoor sporting magazines increasingly include columns detailing cases where people have used guns to protect themselves from criminals or intruders.

Gun control is an emotionally charged issue. Gun control advocates believe guns are killing people. Gun rights activists

Gun owners and supporters participate in the Illinois Gun Owners Lobby Day activities on March 7, 2012, before marching to the state capitol to rally for gun rights.

believe *people* are killing people and need guns to protect themselves. Political parties tend to line up on one or the other side of the argument. Powerful lobbying groups further polarize the nation. Urban and rural citizens face off about gun policies, as do states and the federal government, peace officers, and civilians. And many Americans continue to buy guns and use them through the ongoing stalemate in national policy about gun control.

The City, the Country, and Guns

America's ceaseless gun debate has a great deal to do with geography. The United States is a large nation with many big cities but also sweeping rural areas. The people who live in these environments have very different lifestyles. City dwellers may live in high-rise apartment buildings and use public transportation instead of owning a car. Country dwellers live in houses, sometimes miles away from their neighbors and the nearest town. Few city residents have vegetable gardens or hunt for their food, whereas these activities are common among country residents. City residents may have little use for guns, especially shotguns or rifles, and rarely own them. Country residents may own several guns, particularly shotguns and rifles, and use them frequently as tools for maintaining their lifestyle. Because people in the country have positive or useful purposes for guns, they are more likely to oppose restrictions on gun ownership. A far smaller percentage of city residents is likely to use guns for things like target shooting and hunting, and because many of them see guns as having a mostly negative and dangerous purpose, such as being used to commit crimes, city residents are more likely to favor restrictions on gun ownership.

No Easy Answers

"One thing there is consensus on is guns increase the lethality of violence. There's less agreement on whether guns lead to more violence or less. . . . It's a very difficult question to answer with scientific certainty."—Daniel Webster, codirector of the Johns Hopkins Center for Gun Policy and Research

Quoted in Mayors Against Illegal Guns. "The Arizona Republic." www.mayorsagain stillegalguns.org/html/media-center/ar_071711.shtml.

The demographics of country areas versus city areas explain much of the controversy over gun control in America. Cities are by far the most likely places in the nation for innocent people to be shot. Crime rates vary from city to city and even from area to area within a city, but the CDC reports that two-thirds of all gun homicides in the United States happen in the fifty largest metropolitan areas. Inner-city residents especially tend to support laws that would let fewer people have guns, since in their environment the risk of being shot is twice the national average.

Rural communities, on the other hand, have relatively low crime and murder rates. This is partly because they are not as densely populated—where there are fewer people, there are generally fewer crimes. However, even the per capita crime rate—which adjusts for population density by counting the number of crimes that happen per thousand or hundred thousand residents—tends to be much lower in the country than in the city. Most federal gun control policies, however, limit or restrict access to guns for everyone equally. This is one reason why gun control tends to gain favor in cities but is unpopular in most rural areas.

Unlike their urban counterparts, rural residents often own several types of guns as part of their outdoor lifestyles.

The Politics of Guns

The city-versus-country standoff on gun control seeps into politics, too. Largely based on their constituents, or the voting public they represent, politicians take sides on the gun control debate. "Irrespective of regional and party differences, urban legislators are much more likely to favor gun control measures than are their rural counterparts,"[43] says sociologist Gregg Lee Carter. States that are mainly rural, such as Montana and Alaska, tend to be politically conservative and are more likely to elect officials who are Republicans. States that have large urban populations, like Illinois and California, tend to be politically liberal and elect more officials who are Democrats. Because many Republican politicians represent rural areas with typically higher gun ownership per capita, Republicans have become the political party more likely to support gun rights and oppose gun control. Many Democratic politicians represent urban areas where residents call for stricter gun control measures, so Democrats have become the political party more likely to support gun control. Not all Republicans are pro-gun and not all Democrats are anti-gun, but the political parties are defined in part by how likely they are to favor or oppose taking guns away from citizens. "By the 1990s, gun control had become a beacon to illuminate the difference between the Republican and Democratic Parties,"[44] Carter says.

Political candidates develop what is called a platform when they run for office—a statement of their goals, values, and beliefs. A position on guns has become an important part of this platform, especially for Republicans. A Democrat who does not support gun control may still win the favor of Democratic voters. A Republican who *favors* stricter gun control, however, tends to draw the wrath of Republican voters and is less likely to be elected or reelected to office. Even Democrats often face election struggles if they take a strong position in favor of gun control. During the 2000 presidential election, for example, gun control was a big issue. The Clinton administration had recently passed gun control laws that proved unpopular. Democratic presidential candidate Al Gore ran on a platform that in part favored gun control measures, and this became a heated issue throughout his campaign. Ultimately, voters elected George W. Bush, a candidate with a more gun-friendly platform. Although gun control was not the central issue of that election and is not the primary issue of concern for most voters in any election, political candidates have learned that to strongly favor gun control is to risk losing votes. Few candidates to this day take a strong stand in favor of stricter gun control. "The conventional wisdom has been that supporting gun control can be political suicide,"[45] says law professor and political author Carl Bogus.

States Versus the Federal Government

Gun control is not just about cities versus the country or Democrats versus Republicans. It has also traditionally been part of a larger struggle between states and the federal government. Since the writing of the Constitution, Americans have been at odds about whether state governments or the federal government should have the most power. The initial thirteen colonies had trouble coming together as a nation because some of them preferred to do things their own way and worried about federal power taking over. The American Civil War was in essence fought over the same issue—Southern states wanted the right to govern themselves as they saw fit (which included having slavery), and the federal government wanted to make a single law abolishing slavery, one by which all states in the Union would have to abide.

Gun control, too, is largely a squabble over whether states should be able to make their own gun rules or whether the federal government should make gun laws everyone has to follow. To many Americans, leaving each state to create its own gun laws seems like the most logical choice. If Montana, a state with high gun ownership but very little gun crime, wishes to have lenient gun laws, many people say it should be allowed to do so; whereas if California, which has high gun crime rates, wishes to restrict guns, it too should be allowed to make the laws that best suit its needs. States do have a lot of freedom to pass their own gun laws, such as whether citizens are allowed to carry concealed weapons. But some circumstances seem to warrant federal gun laws that apply equally to all states.

Tragedy Breeds Controversy

After nearly two decades with few new federal gun control laws, a tragedy in Chardon, Ohio, revived the efforts of gun control activists. In February 2012 a student at Chardon High School brought a handgun to campus and opened fire on his classmates, killing three and seriously wounding two others. Almost immediately, gun control and gun rights groups spoke out about the disaster. Gun control activists maintained that it is far too easy for American children and teens to get their hands on firearms, and tragedies like the Chardon shooting are the inevitable outcome. Gun rights activists defended the position that the blame in such tragedies belongs solely to the shooter who uses the gun to carry out his crime. School shootings are horrifying events American families have come to fear. Whether the problem of interpersonal violence between young people can be solved by eliminating guns from society is at the heart of the issue. Every time another school shooting occurs, both sides of the gun control debate seize on it as an example of why their position is right.

Students at Chardon High School in Ohio memorialize victims of a shooting at the school in February 2012. Gun critics believe it is still too easy for children to get guns.

One example of a federal gun control law was the 1938 Federal Firearms Act that outlawed the purchase of a gun by any convicted felon anywhere in the country. If this law did not apply equally to all states, a felon might be able to obtain a gun in one state, then take it into another state that prohibited selling firearms to convicted felons. To make things fair, the federal government passed a single gun law that applied equally to all states. Today, even despite federal laws, states that strictly enforce gun control policies complain that residents of states with more lenient laws carry their guns across state borders, often illegally. "We consistently have criminals purchasing guns in states with lax gun laws," says Kristen Rand, legal policy director of the Violence Policy Center. The guns are then taken to other states like New York, where they are used in crimes. "There is a need for more uniform laws,"[46] Rand says.

Not all Americans agree that tighter federal control of gun sales is the answer to America's gun and violence problems. The federal government is often seen as overstepping its bounds when it passes nationwide laws about education, for example, or health-care reform, things many people think states should decide for themselves. Gun control similarly has become an important issue in the larger debate over whether states or the federal government should be in charge. This, too, divides Americans on their views of gun control. A majority of Americans have a negative view of suggested federal gun control laws like a nationwide ban on handguns, an idea that was favored by only 26 percent of people who responded to a 2011 Gallup poll. Some Americans see such laws as an example of the federal government exerting too much power over states and people. "All too often, Washington imposes mandates and regulations on private activity that many believe would be better left to states and communities to address,"[47] says Peter Roff, a senior fellow at the Institute for Liberty.

Peace Officers

As gun control increasingly becomes a struggle between state and federal governments, it also becomes a fight between local, state, and federal police officers. When federal gun control laws are passed, such as the 1994 Brady Act's requirement to run background checks on anyone who wants to buy a gun, local police agencies must do most of the work of implementing it. This can increase the workload and paperwork burden on local police officers. "Under the Brady Act, state and local law enforcement officers had been forced to spend literally millions of hours investigating handgun buyers,"[48] says attorney and political science researcher David B. Kopel. Local police forces are funded mostly by local taxes such as city and county taxes, so when federal gun control laws make extra demands, local taxes may increase to pay for more police officers to do the work. A majority of people in many states and local communities oppose federal gun control laws for these reasons and prefer to make and enforce their own gun rules.

GUNS AS AN ELECTION FORCE

"A lot of anti-gun advocates have lost their Congressional seats because of their support for more gun control. That fact was not lost on either party in the [2006] election. Democrats realize that gun control is a losing issue with much of the electorate, particularly with the union and blue collar workers they claim as their political base."—Idaho senator Larry Craig

Quoted in Katie Couric. "10 Questions: Opposing Gun Control." CBS News, April 27, 2007. www.cbsnews.com/8301-500803_162-2734640-500803.html.

Local police also tend to favor gun rights for citizens because they realize they cannot prevent every crime from happening. In the average American community, there are about two police officers for every thousand people, according to the National Association of Chiefs of Police (NACP). Police cannot possibly oversee every citizen at every moment in order to keep people safe. According to the NACP's 2010 national survey, the majority of the country's police chiefs support allowing citizens to carry their own weapons—71 percent affirmed that "qualified, law-abiding armed citizens can be of assistance to the professional law enforcement community in promoting justice and reducing the incidence of violent criminal activity."[49]

On the other hand, the increasing number of armed civilians on the streets does not always make a police officer's job easier. Not everyone who carries a gun is necessarily skilled at using it responsibly, especially in states with few to no training requirements for obtaining a concealed-carry permit. Also, even though states that allow concealed carrying typically restrict it only to people without criminal records or a history of treatment for serious mental illness, police have no way of knowing on sight if a person in public with a gun possesses it legally or not. "If we don't know their mental health background, we're at a disadvantage . . . and if they have the ability to have a weapon it makes our interaction even worse,"[50] says Jimmy Jackson, assistant police superintendent of the Chicago Police Department. Criminals might be committing crimes elsewhere while police are occupied with questioning law-abiding citizens about the guns they are carrying, and some police officers also worry that an increase in armed citizens overall will lead to shootouts in situations where armed criminals otherwise might not have drawn their guns and fired.

Lobbyists at Large

Police officers and civilians alike have varied opinions about whether the nation should have stricter or more lenient gun laws. Groups of citizens who feel strongly about the debate band together to better voice their opinions. As such groups grow in size, they become powerful enough to start persuading elected officials to support their side of the issue. Such groups are known as lobbies. Lobbyists, professional advocates who are hired by lobbies or special interest groups, meet with elected officials or make speeches to government bodies at the local, state, and national level in order to influence government decisions and legislation. According to the Center for Public Integrity, a nonpartisan investigative news organization, there are 145 different groups in America that lobby on the issue of guns. Lobby groups that oppose gun control outnumber those that favor stricter gun laws three to one.

The nation's largest and most powerful lobby in favor of gun control is the Brady Campaign to Prevent Gun Violence,

The Brady Campaign is a gun control organization that lobbies elected officials at all levels of government to pass laws that curtail gun violence. Here, members rally in front of the U.S. Supreme Court building in 2008.

founded in 1974 as the National Council to Control Hand-guns. The organization's name was changed to the Center to Prevent Handgun Violence in the 1990s, and then to the Brady Campaign in 2001 in honor of James Brady, the press secretary who was seriously injured by a gunshot to the head during the attempted assassination of Ronald Reagan in 1981. The Brady Campaign lobbies elected officials at all levels of government—local, state, and federal—to pass laws that cut down on gun violence. According to the organization's mission statement, "We are devoted to creating an America free from gun violence, where all Americans are safe at home, at school, at work, and in our communities."[51] The Brady Campaign supports measures like stricter background checks, bans on assault-style weapons, and laws designed to curb illegal gun trafficking, such as limiting the number of firearms that can be bought in a single purchase. "In America, we make it too easy for dangerous people to get dangerous weapons," says the organization's website. "There are only a few federal gun control laws on the books, and even those have loopholes. This leads to senseless gun violence affecting tens of thousands."[52] The Brady Campaign has twenty-eight thousand members in chapters throughout the country.

Of the numerous lobby organizations that oppose stricter gun laws, the National Rifle Association (NRA) is the largest and most powerful. It was founded in 1871 as a response to all the poorly trained marksmen among Union troops during the Civil War. The organization's original focus was teaching people to use guns, and education has remained its chief goal ever since. NRA instructors train 750,000 gun owners per year in the safe and proper use of firearms. The organization pioneered a gun-safe program in 1988 that has taught 21 million preschool and elementary students to stop, back away, and tell an adult if they see a gun. Claiming nearly 4 million members as of 2011, the NRA actively opposes most proposed laws that might limit the rights of law-abiding gun owners or law-abiding citizens who wish to purchase a gun. According to the NRA website, the organization is "widely recognized today as a major political force and as America's foremost defender of Second Amendment rights."[53]

Gun control activists criticize the NRA, saying it uses its size and its $150 million budget to bribe or bully elected officials into opposing gun control. "In the 2010 election cycle," says psychology professor and political author Drew Westen, "the N.R.A. spent over $7 million in independent expenditure campaigns for and against specific candidates, and it has a remarkable record of success at taking out candidates and elected officials with the misfortune of being caught in its crosshairs."[54] The NRA admits that keeping politicians who favor gun control out of office is one of its missions. "It's bad politics to be on the wrong side of the Second Amendment at election time,"[55] says Wayne LaPierre, NRA executive vice president.

Despite the perception that it bullies political candidates, the NRA has the independent support of a majority of Americans—68 percent of Gallup poll participants view

The National Rifle Association is the largest and most powerful pro-gun lobby in America. The NRA actively opposes most proposed laws that might limit carrying or purchasing guns.

F for Firearms

In 1990 Congress passed the Gun-Free School Zones Act to keep guns out of buildings and off the grounds of schools around the nation. Any adult caught carrying a weapon within the half-mile boundary of a school faces possible jail time, and students caught on campus with a gun could be suspended or even expelled. The CDC estimates that about 135,000 guns may be brought to school campuses every day by students involved in gang activity, students fearful of bullies, and students considering a school shooting. The Gun-Free School Zones Act seemed to supporters like a sensible law to protect children and teenagers from guns. However, as with any gun control measure, it met with controversy. States and communities questioned the federal government's ability to mandate that they follow the new policy, and the Supreme Court decided the requirement was unconstitutional. Today states are allowed to create their own policies. Most follow some version of the act. But even though shooting deaths of children and teenagers may be the most tragic of all gun-related deaths, measures that would help safeguard America's youth while at school still meet with public and legal debate.

Officials investigate a 2011 shooting at an Omaha, Nebraska, high school. The CDC estimates that nearly 135,000 guns may be brought into schools every day in the United States.

the NRA favorably, according to statistics listed on the Gallup website in 2012. This suggests that on the whole, most Americans agree with the aims of the leading organization that works to keep gun laws from passing. Widespread public support of the NRA does affect politicians, many of whom are wary of earning an unfavorable rating from the NRA. "Most have clearly made the risk assessment that they have more to fear from the N.R.A. than they do from an occasional sniper,"[56] says Westen. Perhaps in part because of the influence of advocacy groups like the NRA, public support for fewer and less restrictive gun laws has caused a lull in national gun control legislation since the 1990s.

Guns and Crime—Opposing Trends

Gun ownership, the number of states that allow citizens to carry concealed weapons, and public support for people's right to keep and bear arms have been on a steady rise for decades. During the same time period, crime rates, including crimes committed with guns, have seen a steady decline. These statistics likely explain, at least in part, the public's strong current support for gun rights and opposition to gun control. As criminologists point out, however, national crime tends to rise and fall in cycles. The current decline in crime could shift to an increase. If that happens, public support for gun control will probably gain in strength, as it did in the 1990s.

Whether or not people have easy access to guns seems to have little impact on the nation's crime rates, despite the insistence of gun control advocates that more guns will equal more crime and the argument of the gun rights lobby that more guns will reduce crime. Nevertheless, people who favor gun control continue to fight for the stricter gun laws they feel will make the nation safer, while gun rights supporters continue to fight for fewer restrictions on their right to keep firearms for sport, self-defense, or simply because the Constitution says they can. "The gun issue has been, and will continue to be, one of the nation's most controversial and intractable policy issues,"[57] says Carter.

Gun control continues to divide the country because of the different ways people on opposite sides of the debate identify with political parties, interpret the Constitution, view federal versus state power in government, and assess personal rights and responsibility. Both sides of the debate argue passionately in favor of their case as the battle over guns continues to define generation after generation of American citizens.

Introduction: Murder by Gunfire

1. Quoted in Matthew Jaffe. "Schumer Says Loughner's Drug Abuse Should Have Prevented Gun Purchase." ABC News, January 16, 2011. http://abcnews.go.com/blogs/politics/2011/01/schumer-says-loughners-drug-abuse-should-have-prevented-gun-purchase.

2. Quoted in Nathan Thornburgh. "After Tuscon: Why Are the Mentally Ill Still Bearing Arms?" *Time*, January 10, 2011. www.time.com/time/nation/article/0,8599,2041448,00.html.

Chapter 1: Guns and the Law in U.S. History

3. Gregg Lee Carter. *Guns in American Society: An Encyclopedia of History, Politics, Culture and the Law.* Santa Barbara, CA: ABC-CLIO, 2002, p. 86.

4. Quoted in Paul Halsall. "The Bill of Rights, 1689." *Modern History Sourcebook.* Fordham University, 1997. www.fordham.edu/halsall/mod/1689billofrights.asp.

5. H. Richard Uviller and William G. Merkel. *The Militia and the Right to Bear Arms; or, How the Second Amendment Fell Silent.* Durham, NC: Duke University Press, 2002, p. 12.

6. Quoted in Robert J. Spitzer. *Gun Control: A Documentary and Reference Guide.* Westport, CT: Greenwood, 2009, p. xxiv.

7. James B. Jacobs. *Can Gun Control Work?* New York: Oxford University Press, 2002, p. 20.

8. Harry L. Wilson. *Guns, Gun Control, and Elections: The Politics and Policy of Firearms.* Lanham, MD: Rowman & Littlefield, 2007, p. 11.

9. Duncan Watts. *Dictionary of American Government and Politics.* Edinburgh: Edinburgh University Press, 2010, p. 133.

10. Kristin A. Goss. *Disarmed: The Missing Movement for Gun Control in America*. Princeton, NJ: Princeton University Press, 2006, p. 39.

11. Quoted in Stephen A. Holmes. "Gun Control Bill Backed by Reagan in Appeal to Bush." *New York Times*, March 29, 1991. www.nytimes.com/1991/03/29/us/gun-control-bill -backed-by-reagan-in-appeal-to-bush.html?pagewanted =all&src=pm.

12. Quoted in United Press International. "Brady Law Fails to Reduce Murders," August 2, 2000. http://archive.newsmax .com/articles/?a=2000/8/1/183258.

Chapter 2: Legal Issues in the Gun Control Debate

13. Benedict D. LaRosa. "The Second Amendment Protects an Individual Right." Future of Freedom Foundation. www.fff .org/freedom/0101f.asp.

14. Patrick J. Charles. *The Second Amendment: The Intent and Its Interpretation by the States and the Supreme Court*. Jefferson, NC: McFarland, 2009, p. 23.

15. Theodore L. Johnson. *The Second Amendment Controversy— Explained*. Lincoln, NE: iUniverse, 2002, p. 155.

16. Earl E. Pollack. *The Supreme Court and American Democracy: Case Studies on Judicial Review and Public Policy*. Westport, CT: Greenwood, 2009, p. 374.

17. Quoted in CBS News. "Heated Debate over Assault Weapons," July 26, 2009. www.cbsnews.com/2100-3460_162 -4954990.html.

18. Quoted in NRA Institute for Legislative Action. "Liberals Scramble to Extend Clinton Gun Ban," September 8, 2004. www.nraila.org/news-issues/in-the-news/2004/9/liberals -scramble-to-extend-clinton-gun.aspx?s=%22National %22&st=&ps=.

19. Sarah Thompson. "Raging Against Self-Defense: A Psychiatrist Examines the Anti-gun Mentality." Jews for the Preservation of Firearms Ownership, 2000. http://jpfo.org/filegen -n-z/ragingagainstselfdefense.htm.

20. Spitzer. *Gun Control*, p. 67.

21. Fred E. Foldvary. "Concealed Weapons." Editorial. *Progress Report*, 1999. www.progress.org/fold111.htm.

22. Andrew Rosenthal. "The Gun Lobby and Military Suicides." *New York Times*, November 8, 2011. http://takingnote.blogs .nytimes.com/2011/11/08/the-gun-lobby-and-military -suicides.

23. Gary Kleck. *Targeting Guns: Firearms and Their Control.* Hawthorne, NY: Aldine de Gruyter, 1997, p. 373.

Chapter 3: Arguments in Favor of Gun Control

24. Dennis Henigan. "Thousands Lit Candles Against the Darkness of Gun Violence." *Brady Blog*, Brady Campaign to Prevent Gun Violence, January 11, 2012. http://blog.brady campaign.org/?cat=186.

25. Quoted in David Hemenway. *Private Guns, Public Health*. Ann Arbor: University of Michigan Press, 2004, pp. 119–120.

26. Alan N. Schwartz. "Guns and Suicide." *Dr. Schwartz's Weblog*, Mental Help Net, April 12, 2007. www.mentalhelp .net/poc/view_doc.php?type=doc&id=28649.

27. Quoted in Bonnie Rochman. "A Florida Judge Says It's O.K. for Pediatricians to Ask About Guns." *Time*, September 15, 2011. http://healthland.time.com/2011/09/15/why -its-now-okay-for-pediatricians-in-florida-to-talk-about -guns/#ixzz1yXw7SJls.

28. James Alan Fox. "More Guns Means More Guns." *New York Times*, January 12, 2012. www.nytimes.com/roomfordebate /2011/01/11/more-guns-less-crime/more-guns-means -more-guns.

29. Quoted in Zeke Campfield. "Some Oklahoma Law Officers Wary of 'Open Carry' Bills." *Insurance Journal*, March 27, 2012. www.insurancejournal.com/news/southcentral /2012/03/27/240897.htm.

30. Quoted in Violence Policy Center. "Concealed Handgun Permit Holders Have Killed at Least 151 Since May 2007, Including 9 Law Enforcement Officers." Press release, March 24, 2010. www.vpc.org/press/1003ccw.htm.

31. Adam Cohen. "The Latest Crime-Solving Technique the Gun Lobby Doesn't Like." *Time*, June 18, 2012. http://ideas.time .com/2012/06/18/the-latest-crime-solving-technique-the -gun-lobby-doesnt-like/?iid=op-main-lede#ixzz1y9sz RfqN.

32. Quoted in Liz Foschia. "Tough Prison Terms Don't Reduce Crime: NSW Study." ABC News, March 13, 2012. www .abc.net.au/news/2012-03-13/tough-prison-terms-don27t -reduce-crime3a-study/3886402.

33. Quoted in Brady Campaign to Prevent Gun Violence. "Lawmakers Introduce Bill to Permanently Reinstate Brady Waiting Period." Press release, February 24, 1999. www.brady campaign.org/media/press/view/164.

34. Sarah Brady. "Sarah Brady to Obama: Lead on Gun Control." CNN, January 19, 2011. www.cnn.com/2011/OPIN ION/01/18/sarah.brady.tucson.shooting/index.html.

Chapter 4: Arguments in Favor of Gun Rights

35. Quoted in Brian Doherty. *Gun Control on Trial: Inside the Supreme Court Battle over the Second Amendment*. Washington, DC: Cato Institute, 2008, p. 30.

36. Clayton E. Cramer and David Burnett. *Tough Targets: When Criminals Face Armed Resistance from Citizens*. Washington, DC: Cato Institute, 2012, p. i.

37. Gary Kleck. *Point Blank: Guns and Violence in America*. New Brunswick, NJ: Aldine Transaction, 2009, p. 238.

38. Steven D. Levitt and Stephen J. Dubner. *Freakonomics: A Rogue Economist Explores the Hidden Side of Everything*. New York: HarperCollins, 2009, p. 150.

39. Wilson. *Guns, Gun Control, and Elections*, p. 6.

40. Quoted in Dan Noyes. "Hot Guns: How Criminals Get Guns." *Frontline*. www.pbs.org/wgbh/pages/frontline/shows /guns/procon/guns.html.

41. Quoted in Adam Liptak. "Gun Laws and Crime: A Complex Relationship." *New York Times*, June 29, 2008. www.nytimes.com/2008/06/29/weekinreview/29liptak .html?pagewanted=all.

42. John Stossel. "Gun Control Isn't Crime Control." *New York Sun*, February 27, 2008. www.nysun.com/opinion/gun-control-isnt-crime-control/71908.

Chapter 5: The Gun Control Battle Rages On

43. Carter. *Guns in American Society*, p. 138.

44. Carter. *Guns in American Society*, p. 138.

45. Carl Bogus. "How Gun Control Got Murdered." *American Prospect*, August 30, 2012. http://prospect.org/article/how-gun-control-got-murdered.

46. Quoted in Brian Robinson. "Trafficking Fueling Gun Check Problems." ABC News, March 22, 2012. http://abcnews.go.com/US/story?id=93758&page=1#.T-uQqlKClHI.

47. Peter Roff. "Poll: Most Americans Think the Federal Government Has Too Much Power." *U.S. News & World Report*, August 25, 2011. www.usnews.com/opinion/blogs/peter-roff/2011/08/25/poll-most-americans-think-the-federal-government-has-too-much-power.

48. David B. Kopel. "The Brady Bill Comes Due: The *Printz* Case and State Autonomy." *George Mason University Civil Rights Law Journal*, Summer 1999, pp. 190–191.

49. National Association of Chiefs of Police. "22nd Annual National Survey Questions," 2010. www.nacoponline.org/22nd.pdf.

50. Quoted in *Huffington Post*. "Chicago Police Officers Voice Concerns over Illinois Concealed-Carry Bill," April 21, 2011. www.huffingtonpost.com/2011/04/21/chicago-police-officers-v_n_852083.html.

51. Brady Campaign to Prevent Gun Violence. "Mission Statement." www.bradycampaign.org/about.

52. Brady Campaign to Prevent Gun Violence. "Frequently Asked Questions." www.bradycampaign.org/about.

53. National Rifle Association. "Brief History of the NRA." http://home.nra.org/#/nraorg/text/generic_page,3.

54. Drew Westen. "Silencing the Guns." *Campaign Stops Blog*, nytimes.com, March 26, 2012. http://campaignstops.blogs.nytimes.com/2012/03/26/silencing-the-guns.

55. Quoted in Erika Werner. "Obama Gun Control Policy: President Stays Virtually Silent on Issue." *Huffington Post*, November 25, 2011. www.huffingtonpost.com/2011/11/25 /obama-gun-control-democrats_n_1112979.html.

56. Westen. "Silencing the Guns."

57. Quoted in Spitzer. *Gun Control*, p. xx.

Chapter 1: Guns and the Law in U.S. History

1. How did the Gun Control Act of 1968 differ from the National Firearms Act of 1934 and the Federal Firearms Act of 1938? Which do you think was most successful, and why?

2. What are some similarities and differences between the government's prohibition of alcohol and its efforts to regulate gun ownership in America?

3. What role do you think the Brady Act of 1994 and the Assault Weapons Ban of 1994 had in the historically low crime rates of the period?

Chapter 2: Legal Issues in the Gun Control Debate

1. If you were a Supreme Court justice, would you agree that the Second Amendment gives individual citizens the right to keep and bear arms, or would you say it applies only to a militia? How would you defend your decision?

2. What are some possible pros and cons of requiring background checks and waiting periods for gun purchases?

3. The author says gun rights activists see taxing ammunition as a sneaky form of gun control. Do you think ammunition taxes are ethical gun control measures, or are they underhanded? Explain your reasoning.

Chapter 3: Arguments in Favor of Gun Control

1. How do the United States' crime statistics compare with those of other developed countries? How do you think the presence of guns affects these statistics?

2. Is there ever a good reason to equip guns with features like laser sights or silencers? Give reasons to support your answer.

3. Do you think keeping a gun in the home makes the home safer or more dangerous for the people who live there? Why?

Chapter 4: Arguments in Favor of Gun Rights

1. Statistics show that accidental gun deaths make up a small percentage of all accidental deaths. Does this mean gun accidents are no cause for worry in America? Give reasons for your answer.

2. If all guns were banned in the United States, what might the consequences be for law-abiding citizens? For criminals?

3. What do you think of the notion that the government wants to control American citizens by taking away their right to own weapons?

Chapter 5: The Gun Control Battle Rages On

1. Would it be better for the federal government to pass national gun laws for all the states to follow, or should states make their own laws with no national regulation of guns whatsoever? Should there be a mix of both? Defend your opinion.

2. Imagine you were a police officer. Make an argument for or against laws to allow armed citizens in the public spaces of your community.

3. If a Gallup poll asked your opinion of the National Rifle Association, how would you answer and why?

ORGANIZATIONS TO CONTACT

Brady Campaign to Prevent Gun Violence
1225 Eye St. NW, Ste. 1100
Washington, DC 20005-3991
Phone: (202) 898-0792
Fax: (202) 371-9615
Website: www.bradycampaign.org

As a leading organization against gun violence in America, the Brady Campaign works toward the goal of safety at home, at school, at work, and in our communities. The organization works to pass and enforce sensible federal and state gun laws, regulations, and public policies by engaging in grassroots activism, electing public officials who support commonsense gun laws, and increasing public awareness of gun violence.

Bureau of Alcohol, Tobacco, Firearms and Explosives (ATF)
99 New York Ave. NE
Washington, DC 20226
Phone: (800) 800-3855
E-mail: atftips@atf.gov
Website: www.atf.gov

This law enforcement agency protects communities from violent criminals, illegal use and trafficking of firearms and explosives, arson, bombings, acts of terrorism, and the illegal dispensing of alcohol and tobacco products. The ATF strives to safeguard the public with information, training, research, and technology.

Citizens Committee for the Right to Keep and Bear Arms
Liberty Park
12500 NE Tenth Pl.
Bellevue, WA 98005

Phone: (800) 486-6963
Fax: (425) 451-3959
E-mail: adminforweb@ccrkba.org
Website: www.ccrkba.org

The committee is dedicated to protecting Americans' firearms rights. It educates activists, the public, legislators, and the media and helps all Americans understand the importance of the Second Amendment and its role in keeping Americans free.

Coalition to Stop Gun Violence (CSGV)

1424 L St. NW, Ste. 2-1
Washington, DC 20005
Phone: (202) 408-0061
E-mail: csgv@csgv.org
Website: www.csgv.org/index.php

The Coalition to Stop Gun Violence seeks to secure freedom from gun violence through research, strategic engagement, and effective policy advocacy. It consists of forty-eight national organizations working together to reduce gun violence.

Gun Owners of America

8001 Forbes Pl., Ste. 102
Springfield, VA 22151
Phone: (703) 321-8585
Fax: (703) 321-8408
Website: www.gunowners.org

Gun Owners of America is a nonprofit lobbying organization formed in 1975 to preserve and defend Second Amendment rights.

National Rifle Association (NRA)

11250 Waples Mill Rd.
Fairfax, VA 22030
Phone: (800) 672-3888
Fax: (703) 267-3976
Website: www.nra.org

Since 1871 the NRA has focused on firearms education and training for American citizens. Today it is widely recognized as a major political force, America's foremost defender of Second Amendment rights, and the premier firearms education organization in the world.

Violence Policy Center

1140 Nineteenth St. NW, Ste. 600
Washington, DC 20036
Phone: (202) 822-8200
Website: http://vpc.org

The Violence Policy Center is a national nonprofit organization based in Washington, D.C. It works to stop death and injury through research, advocacy, education, and litigation. The center approaches gun violence as a public health issue, advocating that firearms be held to the same health and safety standards that all other consumer products must meet.

Books

David Barton. *The Second Amendment*. Aledo, TX: Wallbuilders, 2000. This book describes the Second Amendment, relates its history, and discusses its controversial meaning regarding the ownership of firearms.

Angela Valdez, John E. Ferguson Jr., and Alan Marzilli. *Gun Control*. 2nd ed. New York: Facts On File, 2011. The authors give pros and cons of government control over firearms and explore some of the major questions that have surrounded guns and the Second Amendment.

Adam Winkler. *Gunfight: The Battle over the Right to Bear Arms in America*. New York: Norton, 2011. The role of and debate over guns in the twentieth and twenty-first centuries is related, including discussions of how guns played into the civil rights movement and dramatic stories of gun control activists and gun rights lobbyists in recent decades.

Internet Sources

Paul M. Barrett. "Gun Control: A Movement Without Followers." *Bloomberg Businessweek*, January 5, 2012. www.business week.com/magazine/gun-control-a-movement-without-fol lowers-01052012.html#p1. The government has done nothing to enact stricter gun control laws since 2000, which the author explains as a consequence of currently low crime rates and strong public support for gun ownership.

Michael Grunwald. "Tucson Tragedy: Is Gun Control a Dead Issue?" *Time*, January 24, 2011. www.time.com/time/maga zine/article/0,9171,2042357,00.html. This article discusses common controversial proposals for gun control and how the shooting of Representative Gabrielle Giffords in 2011 brought them back to the public's attention.

Adam Winkler. "The Secret History of Guns." *Atlantic*, September 2011. www.theatlantic.com/magazine/archive/2011/09/the -secret-history-of-guns/8608. The beliefs of both sides of the gun control and Second Amendment debates are explained, along with how the issue has affected politics in America.

Natalie Wolchover. "With Weaker Laws, More Guns Are Being Trafficked to Criminals." Business Insider, January 11, 2012. http://articles.businessinsider.com/2012-01-11/home /30615236_1_gun-dealer-gun-policy-crime-gun-traces. The author discusses a major negative effect of weakening gun control laws—dishonorable gun dealers are taking advantage of the looser restrictions and allowing people to buy guns in bulk, then resell them to criminals.

Websites

Gun Control vs. Gun Rights, *Open Secrets* **(blog), Center for Responsive Politics** (www.opensecrets.org/news/issues /guns). This site presents a discussion of gun control laws through time and includes ways the legislation affects the average American.

In the News: Gun Control, CNN (http://articles.cnn.com/key word/gun-control). This site has a database of summaries and links to major news articles on gun control published since 2000. Views of both sides of the issue are represented.

Should Civilian Possession of Handguns and Other Non-hunting Guns Be Banned or Severely Restricted? Balanced Politics.Org (www.balancedpolitics.org/gun_control.htm). Popular reasons to argue in favor of and against gun control are given, along with links to further information about the opposing sides of this issue.

INDEX

A
American Academy of
 Pediatrics (AAP), 65
*American Journal of Public
 Health,* 51
American Police Beat
 (magazine), 62
Ammunition
 controls on purchase of,
  38–39
 microstamping of, 72,
  72
Ammunition cartridges,
 45
Arquebus, *11*
Assault weapons, percentage
 of crimes involving, 31
Assault weapons ban,
 22–24
ATF (Bureau of Alcohol,
 Tobacco, Firearms and
 Explosives), 23

B
Background checks, 20, 21,
 37, 67
Bill of Rights (UK), 11–12

Bill of Rights (U.S.), 13, 27
Brady, James, 20, 21, *21,* 85
Brady, Sarah, 20, 21, *21,* 57
Brady Handgun Violence
 Prevention Act (1993),
 20–21, 83
Breyer, Stephen G., 71
Brown Bess, 10
Bullets. *See* Ammunition
Bureau of Alcohol, Tobacco,
 Firearms and Explosives
 (ATF), 23
Bureau of Justice Statistics,
 U.S., 31, 48, 61, 68
Bush, George W., 80

C
Cannons, 10
Center for Public Integrity,
 84
Center to Prevent Handgun
 Violence, 20, 22, 85
Centers for Disease Control
 and Prevention (CDC), 47,
 77–78, 88
Chardon High School
 shooting (OH, 2012), 81

Civil rights movement, 16
Clinton, Bill/Clinton
  administration, 22, 25,
  79
Columbine High School
  shooting (CO, 1999), 56
Concealed-carry policies, 19,
  33–34, 36
  "may issue" *vs.* "shall issue,"
  35
Crime/crime rates
  assault weapons ban and,
    23–24
  Brady Act and, 22
  during Prohibition, 15
  gun control/access to guns
    have little impact on,
    91
  laws prohibiting guns will
    not deter, 60–61
  more guns would not
    increase, 67–68
  percentage involving assault
    weapons, 31
  rural *vs.* urban, 77–78
  violent, percentage
    involving firearms, *60*

D
Deaths
  accidental, 41, 47–48,
    65–67
  due to injury by firearms,
    by state, *49*

See also Homicides/
  homicide rates; Suicide
Delahanty, Thomas, 20
District of Columbia v. Heller
  (2008), 29–30, 61, 71

E
Etheridge, Melissa, 55

F
Federal Bureau of
  Investigation (FBI), 22, 69
Federal Firearms Act (1938),
  15–16, 82

G
Giffords, Gabrielle, 6, 8
Gore, Al, 79–80
Government
  federal, gun control and,
    53–54
  forming militias to protect
    against abuses of, 53–54
Gun Control Act (1968),
  18–19
Gun control/gun control
  laws
    argument for strengthening,
      54, 56–57
    do not deter suicides, 62,
      64–65
    opposition to, 71, 73
    politics of, 79–80
    as racist, 17

rural *vs.* urban split on, 77–78

state *vs.* federal government and, 80, 82

will not deter crime, 60–61

Gun-Free School Zones Act (1990), 88

Gun ownership
personal safety and myth of, 48–50
in U.S., 41–42, 54

Gunpowder, 9–10

Guns
accessories increasing lethality of, 45
accidental injuries/deaths from, 47–48
argument against public carrying of, 50–54
automatic *vs.* semiautomatic, 30
development of, 9–12
percentage of suicides involving, 45
sources of, for felons, 68–69
straw purchases of, 30

Gunshot wounds, 43

H

Handguns, 31–32, *32*

Heller, Dick, 29

Heller, District of Columbia v. (2008), 29–30, 61, 71

Hinckley, John, Jr., 20

Home break-ins, use of guns in protecting against, 48–50

Homicides/homicide rates
Brady Act and, 22
lifting of assault weapons ban and, 24
percentage committed with handguns, 31
in U.S. *vs.* other countries, 41, 42

K

Kennedy, Robert F., 17, *18*

King, Martin Luther, Jr., 17

Ku Klux Klan, 17

L

LaPierre, Wayne, 86–87

Law Center to Prevent Gun Violence, 41

Loughner, Jared, 6–7

M

Martin, Trayvon, 44

Mass shootings, 56, 75

Microstamping, 72

Miller, Jack, 28

Miller, United States v. (1939), 28

Million Mom March, 55, *55*

Murders. *See* Homicides/homicide rates

N
National Association of Chiefs of Police (NACP), 83
National Council to Control Handguns, 84–85
National Firearms Act (1934), 15–16, 28
National Institute of Justice, 67, 68
National Institutes of Health (NIH), 41
National Rifle Association (NRA), 31, 86–89

O
O'Donnell, Rosie, 55
Opinion polls. *See* Surveys
Oswald, Lee Harvey, 17

P
Palmer, Tom, 61
Polls. *See* Surveys
Prohibition, 14–15, 16

R
Reagan, Ronald, 20, 85
Revolutionary War, 13, 58

S
Safety, personal, myth of gun ownership and, 48–50
Sarandon, Susan, 55
Schumer, Chuck, 7

Second Amendment, 13–14, 25–27
Self-defense
argument against use of guns for, 48–50
argument favoring use of guns for, 61–62, 74
Sirhan, Sirhan, 17–18
Stand your ground laws, 44
States
deaths due to injury by firearms by, *49*
federal government *vs.*, in gun control debate, 80, 82
prohibiting concealed carrying of guns, 35
proposing taxes on ammunition, 39
Suicide, 54
presence of gun in home facilitates, 45–47
stricter gun laws do not deter, 64–65
Supreme Court
on Gun-Free School Zones Act, 88
Second Amendment rulings of, 27–29
Surveys
on concealed carrying of guns and feeling safe in public, 52
on National Rifle Association, 87, 89

on nationwide handgun ban, 82
of police chiefs on carrying of weapons, 83

T
Thompson submachine gun (Tommy gun), 15, *15*

U
United Nations International Homicide Statistics, 42
United States, gun ownership in, 41–42

United States v. Miller (1939), 28

V
Virginia Polytechnic Institute shooting (2007), 56

W
Waiting periods, 20, 21, 36–38, 56–57
opposition to, 73
Wild West, 14

Z
Zimmerman, George, 44, *44*

PICTURE CREDITS

ABOUT THE AUTHOR

Jenny MacKay is the author of seventeen nonfiction books for kids and teens on topics ranging from crime scene investigation and sports science to social issues. She lives in northern Nevada with her husband and two children.